Companies don't succeed – people do!

Ideas to create profits through people

Graham Roberts-Phelps

HAWKSMERE

A CRONER.CCH COMPANY

Published by Hawksmere
12-18 Grosvenor Gardens
London SW1W 0DH
www.hawksmere.co.uk

A CIP catalogue record for this book is available
from the British Library.

ISBN 1 85418 109 2

Printed in Great Britain by Ashford Colour Press.

About the author

Graham Roberts-Phelps is an experienced and professional business trainer and consultant, sharing his ideas and insights with thousands of people and organisations every year. With an extensive background in management and business development, he works with organisations of many different types and sizes.

Graham is the author of *Working Smarter* and *Telephone Tactics*, both published by Hawksmere.

Introduction

This book is about how to achieve greater business success by getting each and every person in your organisation to be more successful in the jobs they do, every minute of the day. Whilst this would seem to make a great deal of sense, it is not common practice.

Success should be measured in one way – how each person has contributed to attracting and retaining a customer. Everything else is mere detail. This book also includes ideas about customer magnetism and charm.

Many companies find employees are often caring, hard working, conscientious, enthusiastic and committed for most of the day, excluding the eight hours or so they spend at work!

It is anticipated that you, the reader, will initially reject some of the ideas in this book. You may well consider them as fanciful or not appropriate to your business. I had the same reaction.

However, careful thought is required. The world is an ever fast and changing place, with old rules and methods quickly being replaced by more radical regimes. As Ted Turner, head of CNN, once said: 'Lead, follow, or get out of the way'.

Contents

Customer
relationships

One

1 Encourage your customers to be unreasonable

If you accept that the primary function of every business is to get and keep customers, then it follows that meeting customer demands is what you actually do for a living. To beat your competitors, you must meet those demands better than they do. Therefore, by trying to give your customers something extra special every time you come into contact with them, you will raise their expectations and encourage them to seek the same extra special service from your competitors. Your competitors however, will probably think the customer is being unreasonable and refuse! The result: one captive customer and one poorer competitor.

Meeting customer expectations is not the name of the game – exceeding them is. In order to inspire the people who work in your business, aim to deliver the best to the customer at every contact.

Don't wait for your competitors or customers to force you to react; seize the initiative, be bold and be proactive. After all, what is market leadership if it is not ideas and standards?

'The purpose of a business is to find and keep customers – everything else is mere detail.'

2 Give your customers the benefit of the doubt

There are actually some businesses that mistrust their customers – the very people who allow them to be in business at all! Shocked? Don't be – yours is probably one of them!

These businesses do things like demanding receipts for refunds ('I don't believe you bought it here unless you show me a piece of paper').

▶ Outstanding businesses are different

▶ Outstanding customers are different

▶ Outstanding customers seek out outstanding businesses.

Can you imagine how you would react if the next time you complained the customer service person, shop assistant or waiter accused you of lying and making it all up to try and get some kind of special service, or even your money back? You would, of course, be outraged. Why then do you force customers to write in with complaints, produce receipts and fill in long forms to apply for cover under 'conditional' warranty? How about this, the training company that offers a full refund, at any

3

time, on any course or seminar if you are not completely delighted – stay till the end and ask for your money back! How many do – less than one per cent – from thousands of delegates.

Whatever it is your business makes or provides, decide that from now on you will believe that every customer is honest and trustworthy. If one per cent of these people rip you off and take advantage – don't worry – the customers you attract and keep in the meantime will far exceed any losses.

'Quality is productivity.'

FEDERAL EXPRESS MANAGEMENT MANUAL

3 Encourage your customers to complain

What? Actually invite complaints? Certainly!

Remember: only about a quarter of customers at the very most who are unhappy with you will actually let you know. The rest will let all their friends know about it and start buying from someone else. However, if you could encourage this missing 75 per cent to bring their problems straight to you, you would have a chance to solve them and you would probably keep their custom.

Don't fool yourself that just because people don't complain they're happy. Try this exercise: ask ten different people to name an example of poor or indifferent customer service or salesmanship that they have experienced in the last ten years. When they have finished describing their example, ask them simply, 'What did you do about it? Did you complain?', the answer for most of them will probably be 'Nothing'.

How do you increase complaints? Put comment cards everywhere, free phone numbers on everything and talk to customers, ex-customers and non-customers at every opportunity. Make opportunities – hang around – phone them – write to them – anything – just get more complaints.

5

Oh yes, and act on whatever those complaints tell you and don't forget to say 'thank you' to customers who do complain – consider it as free management consultancy!

'Set yourself a target of increasing the number of complaints by volume, and as a percentage of customer transactions by at least 20 per cent!'

4 Develop a customer retention programme

The fact is that if you don't give your customers some good reasons to stay, your competitors will give them a reason to leave.

Don't use the 'can't afford to' maxim. Most surveys across industries show that keeping one existing customer is five to seven times more profitable that attracting one new one.

How many customers have you lost recently?

Customer attrition, or rather the lack of it, is the key indicator in measuring the success of any retention and customer service strategy. However, it is rarely measured to the degree that it should be. Customer attrition is the number of customers who did not renew their relationship in any one trading period, expressed as a percentage of the number of customers at the start of the month.

'Being good enough, is not good enough – give customers a reason to be faithful.'

How to keep a customer for life – give them lots of reasons to stay

- Select the right customers through market research
- Know your purpose for being in business – to attract and keep a customer, everything else is detail
- Move customers from satisfaction to loyalty by focusing on retention and loyalty schemes
- Develop reward programmes
- Customise your products and services
- Train and empower your employees in excellent customer service
- Respond to customers' needs with speed and efficiency
- Measure what's important to the customer – always add value
- Know exactly what customers want in their relationship with you
- Know why customers leave your enterprise by producing customer exit surveys
- Conduct a failure analysis on your enterprise
- Know your retention improvement measures – have a strategy in place.

'Remember that 96% of unhappy customers never complain. But if their problem remains unsolved – they usually tell ten other customers!'

5 Close the customer service department

If you have a customer service department, it might mean that you don't understand what customer service means.

The principles of customer service belong to every department, every employee and every door along the management corridor. Customer service must be deep in the psyche of your business, not written in a box on the organisation chart.

The trouble with having a customer service 'department' is that it can encourage everybody else in the business to dump their problem customers and customer problems onto someone else, abdicating responsibility.

Customers hate this almost as much as the people who work in the customer service department.

9

> 'Customer satisfaction is everybody's job.'

6 Getting and keeping customers

The primary function of every business and of every person within every business is to get and keep customers, everything else is mere detail.

It is not to make money and it is not to manufacture widgets. It is to get and keep customers. Once this is understood and acted upon, the widgets improve and you make the money anyway.

'It takes less effort to keep an old customer satisfied than to get a new customer interested.'

ANON

7 Customer satisfaction is not satisfactory

Nowadays people expect to be satisfied when they give you their custom – satisfaction is a minimum standard.

Think about it: did you do cartwheels when your school report said 'Satisfactory'? Of course not! You wanted remarks like 'Excellent' or 'Exemplary'.

Don't settle for satisfied customers in your business – aim instead to make them astonished! Someone once said that he wanted customers to feel the same way about his company as an audience feels about a great illusionist: 'Wow! I didn't know you could do that!'

How many times did you make someone go 'Wow!' today?

'It is a descending stream of pure activity, which is the dynamic force of the universe.'

KABBALAH

11

8 The answer is 'yes!'

Just for a moment, pretend to be one of your own customers. Ask one of your staff for something unusual, it may be for a product in an unusual colour, or for a product to be delivered or packed in an unusual way. What does your staff member say?

'Sorry, but no?'

'Nobody else has ever asked for that!'

'Not possible'

'Can't do it'

'I am not authorised'

'You'll have to call back'

'That's against our company policy'

'It's not my fault/job/concern'

The right answer to your unusual request would have been either 'Yes' or 'That's an unusual request, I'll find out if we can do it for you'. Your staff should not believe that it is OK to say 'No' to a customer.

If you don't have the authority to say 'yes', you don't have the authority to say 'no'.

'Problems are nothing but wake up calls for creativity.'

ANON

9 Ways to stay close to your customers

Before you ask customers to show loyalty to you, show loyalty to them. Get the people that serve and know your customers to do one or more of the following (remember, to make it meaningful it has to be from a person they know, not a 'corporate' programme):

▶ Show them that you think of them. Send or fax helpful newspaper clippings, relevant cartoons, Christmas and birthday cards. Here's a novel one – send a card on the anniversary of the day they became your customers!

▶ Call or visit to show them what's new. Always check convenience first, and do it when you're in the area and have time. A brief visit or call to let your customers know about something new or different, or leaving a brochure, is a good way to stay in touch.

▶ Follow up the sale with a free gift to enhance the purchase. You should also make a call to see how your product/service is being utilised and to suggest other ways to derive more benefits. Customers often do not use their purchases correctly first time.

▶ Offer 'valued customer' discounts. These can take the form of coupons, letters, or other sales promotions. This not only encourages more orders; it also makes your customers happy to be getting such good deals.

▶ Let customers know that they should contact you when they hire employees so that you can train the new people for free!

▶ Compensate customers for lost time or money, especially if they were caused by problems with your product/service. Use a well thought out 'recovery programme' and stick to it. Better to err on the side of generosity than to lose a customer out of stinginess.

13

- ▶ Be personal. Keep notes in your customer files on every little detail you know – everything from spouse's name to hobbies and especially their behavioural style.

- ▶ Always be honest. Nothing undermines your credibility more severely than dishonesty. Lies have a way of coming back to haunt you. It also makes people dislike their jobs; don't ask them to lie for you or your organisation.

- ▶ Accept returns unconditionally. The few pounds you may lose in the short run are far less than what you gain from acquiring a new customer. For example you might calculate that it costs an average of £25 to correct a customer's problem. The average customer might spend £15,000 per year, so tell your employees, 'Don't quibble'.

- ▶ Honour your customer's privacy. You may possess some knowledge that should be kept confidential. Your ethical standards demand that you keep it that way.

- ▶ Keep your promises. Never promise something that you cannot deliver. This principle applies to little things such as returning phone calls, as well as big things like delivery dates. If you must, 'baby-sit' deliveries and promised service to see that they are realised. Your reputation and good name are on the line.

- ▶ Give feedback on referrals. This is the right way to show your appreciation for the referral. Tell your customer the outcome. This is also a good way to get more referrals without asking for them directly.

- ▶ Make your customers famous for 15 minutes. If your company has a newsletter or web site, ask customers for permission to write about their success with your product/services, then send a copy to your customer. The same can be done for industry publications.

► Arrange periodic performance reviews. You should meet annually with your customers to review their competitive posture in their industry, their satisfaction with your company, and any other concern that may affect business.

► Keep lines of communication open. As in any relationship, assure your customers that you are open to all calls about everything and anything – ideas, grievances, advice, praise, questions etc. This is one way to maintain that all important rapport.

'The discovery of what is true, and the practice of that which is good, are the two most important objects of philosophy.'

VOLTAIRE

15

10 What are others doing?

When doing research, some businesses try to discover what it is that they are not doing for their customers. Sounds good, doesn't it? But some people say it's not enough. They say the most effective sales strategy is to find out what your competitors are doing for their customers.

As they say in the Mafia, 'keep your friends close and your enemies even closer'.

11 How to serve your customers well

Quality doesn't only apply to merchandise. It also means good service and caring about your customers wants and needs. Listed below are five specific steps for taking better care of your customers:

1   Conduct your own survey. Profit from the ideas, suggestions and complaints of your present and former customers. Solicit their ideas for new products and better service.

2   Meet your customers in person. If your business has grown to the point where you spend most of your time in the office or travelling, take the time to talk to the customers who buy and browse. Observe and ask questions. Think like a customer.

3   Check telephone handling. Bad handling can undermine efforts to build a profitable enterprise. Rules of good handling, such as prompt answering and a cheerful attitude of helpfulness are of critical importance. Check on telephone manners periodically by having someone whose voice is unfamiliar play the role of a customer, perhaps a difficult one.

4   Make it a team. Continually drive home the crucial message that everyone is part of the success machine. Build customer consciousness throughout your organisation. When you hold group meetings, invite ideas from everyone and discuss those ideas.

5   Take advantage of after-hours influence. This is the time when you build, in an informal way, the friendly feeling that draws people to you and your business. Turn friends into customers and reinforce customer loyalty. Take advantage of the relaxed atmosphere of a game of golf, a cocktail party or just a neighbourly chat.

17

12 Free market research

Many sales oriented businesses say that the best market research is a real salesperson asking a real prospect to buy. If there is a sale, find out what made it possible. If there was not a sale, discover why not.

'Every sales call is a free market research opportunity.'

13 Realities of customer-driven service

Customers are changing, your competitors are changing and your staff are changing their expectations. Study the table below and ask yourself which sides of the line you fall:

Factor	Yesterday's business	Today's enterprise
Priority of service	Nice-to-have or necessary evil	A top management concern
Method of service	Corrective action	Customer-driven service management
Customer requirements	Unknown or assumed	Researched and pulsed on a regular basis. Used as basis for decisions
Strategies and systems	Serve organisational and/or internal quality needs	Serve customer needs by doing things right
Management style	Organisational focus; costs and productivity are a top priority	Customer-driven; focused on learning and meeting customers requirements
Responsibility for customer-driven service	Entry-level help trained in tasks, not in service quality delivery	Everyone empowered and trained to serve customer – either external or internal
Motivation and recognition	Rewards are occasional, unplanned and informal	Rewards, recognition and celebrations; regular, planned and public
Performance measurement	Service quality can't be measured	Customer-centred goals and measures, written and publicly displayed, interactive
Communication and feedback	Top down	Interactive

19

14 The customer is not always right

Just to set the record straight, the customer is not always right. But the customer doesn't have to be right. Right or wrong isn't the issue, the issue is: the customer is always the customer and without her or him, you may as well not bother coming to work in the morning.

15 Carefully manage your customer expectations: then exceed them

It is often thought that customer expectations are relative to the price paid for a product or service. In essence, you get what you pay for. However, customers often have higher expectations.

If you really want to be an outstanding business, you must organise your business so that your customers believe that you always give them more than they pay for. These are known as 'moments of truth', where expectations are exceeded and customer delight is achieved.

Because customers measure everything (unconsciously) and little things often matter the most, achieving these 'moments of truth' is both easy and elusive at the same time.

Some suggestions for creating 'moments of truth':

▶ Pay attention to small details – they are the most important ones

▶ Pay attention to the peripheral functions – reception areas, phones, staff manners, parking, customer areas, stock, presentation, letterheads, invoices, packing etc

▶ Everything counts – each time you meet or contact (or don't contact!) the customer, your status in the mind of that customer is either improving or diminishing

▶ Customers want two things: being made to feel special and solutions to problems; so treat every customer as your most important

▶ When you are talking to a customer – they are your most important customer

▶ You only have one customer – the one you are dealing with now

▶ Think of the value of a ten year customer

▶ You might have hundreds of customers – but they might have only one supplier or a one-off purchase

21

- ▶ The world is full of mediocrity – any simpleton can make something a little cheaper but it takes vision and commitment to make or do something better
- ▶ Don't do anything if you can't do it excellently
- ▶ Set or establish clear expectations – and then exceed them
- ▶ Explain terms, prices and conditions clearly, early and honestly
- ▶ Suggestion: build a 10 per cent cushion into all your promises, quotes and statements of performance
- ▶ Deliver faster, sooner, better, cheaper – 10 per cent more that you promised. Don't be tempted to relax or pocket the 10 per cent difference. There is an old farming saying: 'You can shear a sheep many times, but skin it only once'
- ▶ Whatever the customer asks for, the answer is 'Yes!'
- ▶ Do something extra as standard.

'Under promise, over deliver.'

16 Wash your dirty laundry in private

When solving a problem in front of a customer, outstanding employees and managers should never argue or try to apportion blame. Customers should only witness the straight, simple resolving of the problem. Fault-finding is never relevant. Your first priority should always be your customer.

23

17 How much can a junior spend to keep a customer?

It's late at night and only the junior is in your office. The phone rings. It's your best customer and he's angry about something. He will stay angry and will probably cease to be a customer unless he gets a special delivery right now. The cost is £2,000. You're away for three days and can't be contacted. What does the junior do? The only right answer is 'Arrange the special delivery'. Maybe you should tell everyone in your company that it is OK to spend money if it means keeping a customer. Do it now, before it's too late!

'It costs seven times more to win a new customer than to keep an existing one.'

18 Love is... cuddling your clients

Some of the nicest places to work are those where people value close relationships with their clients; they treat them like friends.

Try it and you'll be surprised at the results. Next time one of your clients rings with a problem or a complaint, find the opportunity to sit down together (preferably on the same side of the table) and work out the solution. Then go for a drink together. Before you know it, you will be friends.

19 The three 'R's of customer service

What do customers expect from you and your company?

The vital elements that every interaction with a customer entails consist of three basic components – the three 'R's of service:

1 Reliability

There are several faces to reliability: fulfilling promises, creating realistic expectations, delivering quality products and being dependable.

▶ Organisational reliability

Product or service quality; efficient dependable operational systems; policies and procedures that consistently serve the customer; quality employee training; creating realistic expectations with accurate customer education and communication.

▶ Personal reliability

Timely follow-up on all matters; product knowledge; integrity; and overall professionalism.

2 Responsiveness

Responsiveness includes the willingness to incorporate flexibility in the decision-making; giving a higher priority to customers' needs than to company operational guidelines; and timeliness.

▶ Organisational responsiveness

Structuring company policies and operational procedures so that employees can respond to and serve customers in a timely manner. This requires management to empower employees with the authority to give customers what they want, within reasonable parameters. The decision-making process must be moved as close to the customer as possible.

▶ Personal responsiveness

The willingness and ability to work the system on behalf of the customer. Sales people and other employees must be willing to take the responsibility for customers' problems and, if necessary, sell their solutions upstream.

3 Relationship

Building a positive, loyal, long-term business relationship is important.

▶ Organisational relationship

Focusing on building long-term relationships rather than one-time sales; market research and customer perception research which determines what is important to your target markets; determining and administering guarantees and warranty policies.

▶ Personal relationship

In a nutshell, treating people well. This includes courtesy, recognition, caring, empathy, sincerity, ethical selling, building rapport, establishing trust, and communicating effectively.

The three 'R's in your business

Refer back to the three 'R's of customer service. Then give two examples for each of the specific aspects of reliability, responsiveness, and relationship that are important to your customers.

27

Innovation

Two

20 If it ain't broke – try breaking it

Most people say: 'If it ain't broke, don't fix it'. In a corporate organisation sense this is a recipe for extinction. It is the same as saying, 'We've always done things this way and we're not going to change'. Why not try breaking something tomorrow?

Take a system, department or a team and change it around. Set new objectives (better still, ask the people involved to set their own and encourage intelligent experiments). Make it very clear that mistakes are alright; in fact you expect them with experiments, and watch what happens. Entire businesses have been created in this way.

The only reason companies aren't successful tomorrow is because they are successful today. Intel was a mediocre, struggling manufacturer in the early '70's who saw opportunities that other much larger and more successful companies missed. Have you ever wondered why so many marketing innovations come from small companies and up-start entrepreneurs? For example, Rank Xerox shelved the icon-based system that it developed, only to watch Apple and Microsoft make billions. James Dyson, the inventor was turned away by over forty manufacturers, and was forced to risk bankruptcy to set up his own business that today makes him one of the UK's top-earning multi-millionaires.

21 Benchmark the best, not the average

Do every bit of what you do as well as the best people do it.

Every task your business undertakes has a number of parts. You may be a car repair shop, but you share a part of the job with, for example, British Airways: you both need to provide facilities in which your customers can wait awhile.

If you want to be thought of as the world's greatest car repair shop and delight your customers, even while they're waiting, why not take a look at the BA Executive lounge at Heathrow and model your reception on that?

If you are going to compare against industry standards – aim for the best, not the average. Seek out the best of the key components of your business; who treats their staff the best, despatches and distributes, handles complaints, manages costs and suppliers, innovates, communicates with customers the best etc.

Most industries and businesses play it safe and perpetuate more of the same. This is the most dangerous thing you can do.

31

'If your head's in the sun and you're sitting on a block of ice – your average body temperature is probably okay – but the average is a useless measure!'

22 Good companies are led by visionary champions of change

Vision and change begin at the top. It can be an individual or it can be a team supporting the CEO that champions the continuous change process, but as one individual observed 'they do not manage change: they are change'.

From there the vision is cascaded throughout the organisation so that there are agents of change at all levels, implementing and supporting it. In the best companies change management is not an issue, people expect change. But in all cases the process of change is focused on meeting customers' needs: 'My vision is delighted customers'.

The result is 'undisputed worldwide leadership and profitability'. This vision is not simply focused on tomorrow's customer but addresses issues such as 'What will our customers want to buy in 15 years time?'.

'If one advances confidently in the direction of his own dreams and endeavours to live the life which he has imagined, he will meet with a success unexpected in common hours.'

HENRY DAVID THOREAU

23 Changing your corporate culture

How can we become more _____ focused? (fill in the blank
– customer service, creativity, care, accuracy, etc).

Once you have chosen and launched the programme, highlighting what
you want more and less of, you have to sustain it.

Reinforcement theory tells us that after new behaviour has been established, it can best be perpetuated through intermittent reinforcement.
Translated this means don't forget the behaviour you wanted to have
on an ongoing basis just because a programme to promote it has ended.
Selective encouragement of the behaviour can perpetuate results –
and at a fraction of the original cost. Here are some examples:

▶ Keep communicating about the topic. Carry articles about
continued results and examples of successes in your company
and others. Employee suggestions can continue to be highlighted
by noting company savings from each suggestion or by interviewing
top suggestion makers to encourage role modelling. Management
should also individually thank employees who have continued to
perform as desired.

▶ Provide ongoing training. Emphasise the new behaviours in orientation and training programmes. For example, after the end of a
company-wide quality initiative, be sure the topic of quality is
adequately covered in the new employee orientation programme
as a value the organisation holds dear. Make sure training
programmes are established to continue to promote the desired
skills in practice and to train employees that change jobs or are
new to the organisation.

▶ Align policies and procedures to support new behaviours. Nothing
will kill corporate change programme advances faster than organisational systems that do not support the desired behaviour. For
example, if you have just finished a corporate change programme

that got your sales team focused on selling to larger customers, make sure the company's invoicing system and shipping practices are geared to serving large customers as well.

▶ Hire and promote based upon the valued skills and behaviours of the programme. To perpetuate desired behaviour, make it become a value for the organisation upon which hiring and promotions are based. For example, at Disney they hire employees who are people-oriented, for almost every position in the organisation. By hiring based upon that value, they find it is easier to deliver a better service to customers and perpetuate the service value in their organisational culture. A truly integrated value should also become part of employee performance reviews.

▶ Build upon past programmes. Build and learn from previous corporate change programmes to help launch a follow-up programme. For example, turn end-of-programme awards into a tradition by creating annual awards based upon the criteria of the initial corporate change programme. Or, if you have just had a successful programme to promote improved customer service, shift the emphasis to focus on improved internal service between departments.

24 Creative thinking – Disney style!

You are only as good as your last new idea, whether you are trying to design the Walkman of the '90's or a new letter for your next mail-shot campaign.

Walt Disney was an 'idea genius'. He would take three different and very distinct perspectives when building ideas for new film projects, and it has been claimed that this was the approach that made him such a unique talent. He was able to shift his position to look at his project from each of these three different viewpoints, allowing him a depth of appreciation that others literally couldn't see:

Step 1: Open creativity (The dreamer)

Walt Disney had an extraordinary imagination – that is, he allowed his mind to explore ideas that were beyond the ordinary. He would often wake in the middle of the night to change his plans or to make notes or describe his latest 'dream'. The first step of creative thinking is to dream; to create an idea mentally. Walt Disney represented it as finished and complete, with no reference or consideration of the 'how'.

Step 2: The realist

35

After first creating a vision of the entire film, how did Disney avoid the pie in the sky turning to egg on his face? He would take the realist view, balancing money, time and resources against what was technically possible, and what could be done.

Step 3: The customer (critic)

Once he had created the dream of the film and worked out whether the project was realistic, he then took another look at the whole plan through the eyes of a critical or potential customer – 'Was it interesting?' 'Was it entertaining?' 'Was it too similar to something else?'.

Breakthroughs can be achieved by taking the perpetual position of your customers, or prospective customer, to gain new insights and realisations that can often seem glaringly obvious later on.

'Opportunity is often missed because we are broadcasting when we should be tuning in.'

ANON

25 Add one question to the agenda

When you next have an internal meeting about systems, plans or product changes, add one question to the agenda:

'What will this do for my customer?'

If the answer is 'Nothing' or 'It will make things worse', think seriously about disbanding the meeting, abandoning the project and getting your people to spend their time working for the customer instead.

26 Your tired old product may only need a new category

If you have a dried-up, out-of-date product, or one that is insufficiently differentiated from its competitors, try this:

Get some colleagues together, lock yourselves in a room for a day and brainstorm a completely new category for the product. Dream one up. Invent it. Sometimes you can turn a listless performer into a winner by creating a new category in which you have no competition.

27 The enemy within

In 1990 IBM posted the highest profits of any multinational company – $5bn. If you had been a manager or director at the time, what would have been your expectations for next year – $3bn, $4bn, $6bn? In actual fact they fell off a cliff – in 1991 they made $0 profits and in the following four years they lost $23bn before beginning to turn it around. This example is only one of many.

Every two years, one successful multinational business puts together two teams of people. One is made up of staff and managers. The other consists of customers, regular suppliers and other involved outsiders. The task of both teams is to develop a list of ten statements which summarise 'How we do things around here'. The rest of the organisation then develops a plan for attacking each of these core beliefs (or complacency).

The businesses that do this follow a revenue roller-coaster and often experience bewildering and unexpected shifts in the markets and their results.

39

'*Most businesses have more to fear from complacency than their competitors.*'

28 People buy people first and whatever else second

Consider the article below written by the director of a management consultancy:

'My company had obtained a contract to provide consulting services to a relatively small bottling concern. The contract was substantial, amounting to £30,000. The client had little formal education, his business was in bad shape, and in recent years he had made some very costly mistakes.

Three days after we had got the contract, an associate and I were driving out to his plant. To this day I don't know how it started, but somehow we began talking about the negative qualities of our client.

Before we realised it, we were talking about how his own stupidity had brought about the mess he was in, instead of discussing how we could best approach solving his problems.

I remember one remark I made which I thought was particularly clever – "The only thing holding up Mr X is fat!". My associate laughed and came up with an equally choice observation.

The whole drive out we talked about nothing else but the weak idiot we had as a client.

Well, the meeting that afternoon was cold. Looking back I think our client sensed somehow the way we felt towards him. He must have thought, "These people think I'm stupid and all they're going to do for my money is give me some high-sounding talk".

Two days later I got a two-sentence letter from this client. It said "I've decided to cancel our contract for your consulting services. If there is a charge for your services to date, please invoice me".

*Priming ourselves with negative thoughts cost us a £30,000 contract.
What made it even more painful was learning a month later that
he had contacted another consultancy for the same services.*

*We would never have lost him had we concentrated on his fine
qualities, and he has them, most people do.'*

'You must make your mark on this earth, and,
if you have never done so, it is simply because
you have neglected to use the powers you have,
or you have neglected to develop them.'

JOHN HENRY PATTERSON

41

29 How to have instant ideas

Here's one way to free those annoying creative blocks when you just can't think of the answer to a problem.

Instead of trying to write down a list of answers (which are complex) write down a list of objects. Give yourself just one minute to think of as many objects as possible and write them down. Now start connecting the objects you have written down with the problem you had in the first place. Be free and don't worry if the connections are a little silly. Within minutes, your brain will have relished that it's playtime and anything goes, and when anything goes, answers arrive.

Why does this work? It is your unconscious mind that generates ideas and is the creative powerhouse; the logical mind, or left-brain, filters them. By distracting the conscious mind, the sub-conscious mind can go to work.

'I am looking for a lot of men who have an infinite capacity to not know what can't be done.'

HENRY FORD

30 Own one word in the customer's mind

When you're trying to build awareness for your next product, service or brand, you'll find it much easier to get into your customer's mind if you can do it with one word. The Halifax Building Society has done it with 'biggest', Mercedes with 'engineering', TNT with 'overnight' and Microsoft with 'software'. What's your word? Our company's is 'outstanding'.

When your competitor owns a word or a position in the customer's mind, it is futile to try and own the same word. So if you're planning to make a superb car, don't try and steal 'engineering' from Mercedes. Why not move in on 'quiet' or 'comfortable' instead?

31 The 30 per cent rule

No one customer or customer project should account for more than 30 per cent of your annual sales or profits.

Your forecast sales revenue, or sales pipeline should be at least three times greater than you need to meet the business's cash needs.

'30 per cent of customers and products should be from new sources.'

32 The early bird catches the worm

When planning a new product or service, remember that it is usually more effective to be the first than to be the best.

It is much easier to get into the customer's mind first than to try to convince the world that you have a better product than the one everybody knows.

Don't believe it? Try this test:

> Think of the name of the first something in a field. Now substitute the word 'first' for 'leading'. Most times, the names will be the same. For example, the first chain of hamburger restaurants is also the leading chain of hamburger restaurants and the first microcomputer operating system for Intel computers is also the leading microcomputer operating system for Intel computers.

45

'If you can't be best, be first.'

33 What are your service standards?

Use this questionnaire to focus your organisation's attention on the things that matter.

Have you defined a level of service that you strive to deliver? If not, develop standards for the following:

- ▶ How quickly you return phone calls
- ▶ How closely you monitor the timely delivery of products or services
- ▶ How often you keep in touch with customers and prospects
- ▶ How frequently you solicit customer feedback on your products and service quality.

What other aspects of service can you add to this list?

- ▶ List three ways to make it easier for customers to do business with your company.
- ▶ List three ways to streamline the problem-solving process for customers.
- ▶ List three ways to reduce or eliminate any recurring problems that your customers experience with your product or services.
- ▶ What opportunities are presented by the recurring problems? How can you turn unhappy customers into loyal customers?

34

Making sales at all costs can cost you all you make

In the short-term, deep discounting to make sales increases a company's business. However, in the long-term it can actually destroy a business. It is never worth cutting your price to the point of sacrificing your brand. Once you have sold at a lower price, you have educated your customers to believe that your normal price is too high.

47

35 The liquidation list

A liquidation lawyer used to look for seven things when visiting a business, which told him whether the organisation had lost touch with reality and could soon be a candidate for his specialist skills. He would begin in the car park and look for reserved parking spaces and personalised number plates on director's cars.

A fountain and floodlighting outside the building were the next items to be ticked off if spotted. A separate directors' dining room was always an encouraging discovery, especially if it was silver service. Carpets along the director's corridor when the rest of the company had lino were also a good one.

Nameplates (as opposed to job titles) on office doors were also eagerly searched for. The crowning glory, however, would be a helicopter or corporate plane! When he saw one of these (other than at air transport or offshore oil companies), he would rub his hands in glee! If your company can tick off more than five of the above items, maybe you'd better turn to the beginning and read this book again!

36 Make every encounter count

Every time someone in your organisation makes contact with a member of the public, whether by phone, face to face, by letter, or even by driving past them in the company van, an opportunity presents itself to leave a great impression or a lousy one. Some theorists say that the success of any company is measured by the relationship between these great and lousy impressions, and that everyone in your business should relish every encounter with anyone as an opportunity to make a great impression.

37 Details don't make deals

Never get hung up on the details of a deal. Work instead on the bigger relationship between the two parties and you'll make more deals. The world's best deal makers say this: if two people want to do business together, the details will never stop it from happening, but if two people don't want to make a deal, no amount of detail can ever make it happen.

38 Asked any stupid questions lately?

If someone hadn't asked, 'Why should I have to use a keyboard to interact with my computer?', there would be no such thing as a mouse.

If one Saturday morning James Dyson hadn't asked, 'Why does my vacuum cleaner have to have a messy, dusty bag?', he wouldn't have made the invention that he did.

51

39 Selling a 'people programme' to the board

In every employee motivation, incentive, or recognition programme there comes a time when you need to sell to top management the benefits of what you are doing.

For some programmes this is before you start; for others, it is to be able to continue or expand funding. For all, it is to have the support and credibility that comes from top management endorsement. Here are three ways you can influence top management in your organisation about the importance of an employee recognition or incentive plan:

1   **Bottom line benefits**. Probably the best way to influence top management is to demonstrate a bottom line financial impact that will occur from an increase of recognition in your organisation. This is especially true if you have a culture of 'old style' top managers who feel that giving employees a salary cheque should be enough of a reward to get the best effort from everyone.

    Point to the bottom line impact that other companies have obtained from having recognition programmes that helped drive desired performance objectives. Research and statistics will provide credibility to your proposal and make your case seem more factual than opinionated.

2   **Pilot a programme**. You can run a pilot programme and come up with your own result data. This has the advantage of being done with your own employees, performance goals, competitive pressures and managers. You can also influence the success of a pilot programme, by carefully selecting positive, proactive participants and closely monitoring what is done to increase the chances of favourable results.

If either of these approaches fails to convince your management that employee recognition makes sense, get a programme going that doesn't require any funds at all.

3   Instead use **creative, no cost recognition**, such as personal and written thanks, public praise, morale building meetings and information sessions. Track anecdotal success stories and begin a case for broader implementation. You will be surprised at how much you can do with so little, especially if you involve those you are trying to recognise in the process.

53

40 Kaizen

The Japanese have a word for which we have no direct equivalent – 'kaizen'. It means 'constant change and improvement'. It is better to do a thousand things one per cent better, than one thing a thousand per cent better. To Japanese business it is a way of thinking and managing – a way of competing and surviving. Here are some ideas of how it might apply to getting the best out of people:

Techniques for maintaining constant improvement

What stops managers from acting on their best intentions to recognise employees on a more frequent basis? You can raise awareness as to the importance of recognising employees, and you can practice interpersonal skills so that they have the ability and comfort level to recognise others. Yet for more managers than not, the desired behaviour will fall short of their intentions once they get back on the job.

The ratio of success could increase if we were able to find ways to help managers keep their commitment to their own commitment, that is, to develop an individualised strategy and support plan that increases the likelihood that they will do something different. Following are some tactics that I've seen work for managers in various organisations. Try them, adapt them, and combine them as you see fit for your circumstances and the managers you are trying to influence.

Do one thing differently

The best goals are attainable, reasonable goals, so it may be best to suggest to managers that they only focus on doing one thing differently. For example, starting each staff meeting with good news and praising for individuals who deserve it or perhaps reading thank you letters from satisfied customers or employees from other parts of the organisation. Far better to have managers focus on one thing that is then consistently done than a dozen things that all go to the wayside once the managers step back into their old routines. It's estimated that over 90 per cent of our daily behaviour is routine, so don't underestimate the power of selective focus.

Link the activity into your day planner

For many managers, the key to impacting their routine is tying the new behaviour into their current planning and organising system. Most successful managers are highly analytical and task oriented, that is, excellent at getting identified tasks completed on time. The reason they don't recognise their employees more often is that there is not a clear, specific pressure to do so – that is, nothing keeps them accountable. As a result, they gravitate to what has to be done and what they are more comfortable doing.

One way I've broken through to such managers is to get them to think of their people as 'things to do'. Have them add a list of their direct reports to their 'to do' list, with the instructions to check each person off once they catch that person 'doing something right' during the week. The manager can also write reminders in their calendar for future dates, for example employees' anniversary dates of hire with the organisation.

Get the help of others

Many managers get inspired to start a new behaviour and feel it is a personal quest they have to do all on their own. Not true! In fact, they are likely to have better results if they discuss what they are trying to do and involve others with whom they work.

For example, have managers' partner with someone else that they work with for recognition activities. Perhaps this is a colleague they met in a training session or someone from a different area of the company that they want to have a reason to keep in touch with. Have them exchange action plans with specific times for follow-up and discussion of progress made. This person thus acts as a designated monitor, counsellor and enforcer all in one – essentially, a soul mate for acting on the new behaviours. Or at the next staff meeting a manager can say: 'I'm going to be trying some new behaviour and would appreciate feedback from people about it. Specifically, I'm going to be acknowledging people when I see them doing a good job. I'm trying to do this in a timely, specific way. Let me know when I do it right and if you value me doing it'.

Hold 'one-on-one' meetings

One systematic approach for making more time for your people (a top motivator) is to start holding 'one-on-one' meetings. The idea is to set a minimum acceptable standard for 'face' time with each employee. This might be 15-30 minutes at least once every two weeks. That time is the employees' time, to use as they desire, thus the meetings frequently start with the manager asking, 'What's on your agenda?'.

Other techniques can be creative and fun, such as the manager who decided to place five marbles in his pocket and move one to another pocket each time he gave a praising to an employee, with the goal to do five 'praisings' a day. The first day he didn't move any marbles. The second day he began the day more determined and by the end of the day he had transferred three marbles (and spent the close of the day walking around the office, looking for desired behaviour to reinforce!). After several weeks, however, the manager no longer needed the marbles because the activity became a routine part of his job.

56

'If you always do what you've always done, you'll always get what you always got.'

Time management

Three

41 Rise and shine

Some of the world's most successful people and companies don't put their achievements down to clever management techniques or expensive education. Instead, they arrange things so that they get more hours in a day than most other people do. How? By getting out of bed the minute they wake up and immediately concentrating on the present moment. Sounds awful? Think about this: If you stay in bed after the alarm for just ten minutes every morning, you waste one and a half average working weeks every year. That's one whole year in a working lifetime.

If your staff drift in and edge up to the day slowly – watch out! There is a good chance that your people already have more to do than there is time to do it in, and that means starting the day with a sense of momentum.

Research has also shown that most people, with a few exceptions, are generally more 'up' in the first half of the day – more alert, sharp thinking and quick-witted. Get the best out of them by getting them in early and sending them home on time to be with their families. Their children will thank you for it. The chances are that they are coasting by about four o'clock and are either doing low-priority work or are doing high-priority tasks badly or half-heartedly.

'If you waste an hour in the morning you spend all day looking for it.'

42 E-mail

When you think about it, an internal memo or e-mail is like a phone call from someone who doesn't want to talk to you personally.

Why do people do this? To cover themselves? So that you can't argue? Because they're frightened of you? Whatever the reason, some would say that it's nothing to do with outstanding management.

So what is wrong with e-mail? Nothing in theory, however, to send 100 memos takes time and 100 envelopes; 100 e-mails takes one click. Hence, people are now deluged with a copy of what everybody else is doing. Fifty or more e-mails a day – just from within your own company – are not uncommon.

The solution? Cherry-pick – be very selective about what you read, send and reply to. Prioritise ruthlessly. Worried about missing something? Don't be. After all, if it's that important, they will find a way to talk to you.

Spend the time you save networking, talking, planning, breaking rules and being creative.

59

'However many e-mails or memos you send
– it's probably too many.'

43 No more monkey-management

Problem solving and saving time

Managers often spend an inordinate amount of their day wrestling with problems from subordinates who often aren't even sure what the problems are. So much time is spent sorting out the details of a supposed problem and negotiating its resolution that managers fail to do their own work, and the organisation suffers.

If you find yourself in this situation, use the following approach. Odds are that the time you spend managing 'problems' will dramatically decrease.

Problem solving approach

1 Define the problem precisely. Be exact and succinct.

2 List all of the possible solutions (or some ideas) to the problem.

3 Which of the above is the best solution? Why?

4 If you still need my counsel, you're welcome in my office at any time.

44 Priorities and strengths

Always ask yourself, 'What is the most valuable use of my time right now?'.

If you are always focusing on your top priorities, it is much easier to get other people in the organisation focusing on theirs. If you are not concentrating single-mindedly on the most important thing to be done, it is almost always a recipe for failure. People follow the leader, even if it's to nowhere in particular!

Finding your strengths

Answer the following questions, all of which will help you identify your strengths and your priorities:

▶ What are you good at?

▶ What is your company good at?

▶ What percentage of your day is spent doing what you are good at?

▶ What can you do to begin spending more time doing things you are good at?

▶ If you could give up one part of your job, what would it be?

61

'The great thing in this world is not so much where we are but in what direction we are moving.'

OLIVER WENDELL HOLMES

45 The KISS principle

Try spreading the KISS (Keep it Short and Simple) principle.

For example, it is a waste of time holding a meeting if the matter can be resolved by a quick phone call. There is no point in writing a ten-page report where two pages are all that is necessary and if you do have to send a memo, make sure it isn't to someone you bump into several times a day. For example:

▶ Limit all written reports, letters, memos etc to one side of A4 (it can be done!)

▶ Limit all e-mails to a paragraph

▶ Never use a long word where a short one will do

▶ If it is possible to cut out a word always cut it out

▶ Never use the passive where you can use an active

▶ Never use a foreign phrase, a scientific word or a jargon word if you can think of an everyday English equivalent

▶ Set meetings to finish 25 per cent shorter than is comfortable or normal

▶ Ask people to summarise – 'Give me that in a sentence – 20 words – or less'.

'Everything should be made as simple as possible, but no simpler.'

EINSTEIN

46

Boost your profits with Pareto's Law

Pareto's Law is about concentrating on what is important. Stated simply: the significant items in any group normally account for a relatively small proportion of the total. For example, 80 per cent of your sales probably come from 20 per cent of your customers. Therefore, concentrating most energy on this 20 per cent will bring you the best results.

Applying the rule

How does the maxim rule apply to your customer? It is almost certain that your profitability depends mainly on your ability to satisfy just 20 per cent of your customers. You can't of course forget the other 80 per cent completely. But you would need more than a 24-hour day to put equal emphasis to their demands. The 80/20 rule can be used to identify new business prospects. Analysing the top 20 per cent of your customers should enable you to determine which businesses, or types of business, you need to target to win the best quality new clients.

Improve cash flow

On the accounts side, 80 per cent of the money you are owed will probably be due from only 20 per cent of your customers. In this instance, it is critical to chase large outstanding bills first, rather than going methodically through customer invoices from A to Z, irrespective of the amount owed.

63

One technique that I use is to put annual pound value on the decision. For example, a decision that can save you £100, but which will recur once a week (£5,200 annual savings) is far more important than a decision on £1,000 in an isolated situation that will not recur.

Manage your time

You can apply Pareto's law in your workplace where hundreds of things need your attention! Some things are very important, some less so, and others are worthless. Part of making the law work for you is learning how prioritising means deciding the order in which jobs should be done, and how much time to allocate to each. It is distinguishing between urgent and important tasks. Being urgent does not make something important. Urgent jobs don't always have the highest pay off. They are often unplanned and generally get priority over important jobs. If you're honest, you'll probably find you spend 80 per cent of your time achieving 20 per cent of your goals – leaving just 20 per cent of your time to achieve 80 per cent of your goals. This is madness and obviously bad business sense.

Once you're skilled in this technique, you will find yourself spending more time on the important things. It's not easy and you may have to do some careful planning initially. But once the processes and mechanisms are in place, you'll end up being able to concentrate on the vital parts of the business.

'One always has time enough, if one will apply it well.'

GOETHE

47 How to use time profitably

Think of time in small parcels. Handle small tasks while you are waiting for appointments, standing in queues or jammed in traffic. Carry a pocket recorder for inspirational moments while travelling.

There simply is not enough time to do everything. We all know this is true, and yet our behaviour at work often suggests that we believe there actually is time to do everything. This is the case when we do 'the quick, the easy, the interesting, the fun and the enjoyable', regardless of their urgency and importance. Not only is there not enough time to do every-thing, not all of the time we have is controllable. Some of it is uncontrollable in that the time is not available to work on actions from the to-do list.

65

'The best time to complete your daily plan is the night before. That way you'll wake up motivated and you won't be floundering around for half a day just defining what you want to accomplish.'

TOM HOPKINS

48 Play BANJO everyday

Bang A Nasty Job Off

Instead of leaving the unpleasant tasks and doing the nice ones, be determined to do one nasty job each day. You'll feel wonderful afterwards and you'll be in a much better frame of mind for the tasks you like. Eventually you won't have a pile of ancient papers staring at you every morning either!

'Do a disagreeable job today instead of tomorrow. You will save 24 hours of dreading to do it, while having 24 hours to savour the feeling that the job is behind you.'

ANON

49

Have you got a 'ring, ring, ring' through your nose?

It's easy to become a slave to the ringing phone. Most people answer too many calls and spend too long on the important ones. Try delegating more calls. If you have important work to do, do it, and tell people, 'I'll call you back between 3.30 and 3.45 this afternoon' and always keep your promises.

Stop asking people to call you back – all you are doing is creating more interruptions in your day and inconveniencing them.

50 How to put off procrastinating

Firstly, understand your illness. For procrastination to flourish there are two essential conditions:

1   Spare time in the future (however imaginary).

2   Something more pleasurable to do now (however unimportant).

Now the cure:

1   Do it. Nasty jobs are like jumping into a cold swimming pool; the longer you leave it, the worse it gets, so jump in now, do something, and make a start.

2   Little and often. Everybody leaves nasty jobs to be done in large blocks. Don't let this happen. Integrate small boring tasks with more enjoyable work and make a routine of jobs you regularly procrastinate. Don't allow a series of ten minute nasty jobs to turn into an entire day of misery.

Procrastination is the thief of time!

PROCRASTINATOR'S CREED:

'I will never rush into a job without a lifetime of thought.

I truly believe that all deadlines are unreasonable regardless of the amount of time given.

I shall always begin, start, initiate, take the first step, and/or write the first word, when I get around to it.'

51 Reduce the time you spend in meetings

Meetings cause more lost production than illness, strikes or even bank holidays.

Limit or ration meetings in your organisation and use this one question to weed out the necessary from the indulgent:

'Do we need to make a decision at this proposed meeting?'

If the answer is 'Yes', the get together may be necessary. But if the meeting is only a discussion forum, it's probably a waste of time, so stay away, do something more productive instead and encourage others to join you.

Dos and don'ts of meetings

- ▶ DO – set a timed agenda and keep to it
- ▶ DO – address issues that are relevant to your staff
- ▶ DO – use it as a chance for people to get to know each other and swap ideas
- ▶ DO – make sure people leave the meeting feeling more positive than when they came in
- ▶ DON'T – criticise individuals in public
- ▶ DON'T – talk more than you listen

69

- ▶ DON'T – allow it to become a forum for complaining
- ▶ DON'T – overrun on time
- ▶ DO – follow-up on actions and make sure things get done
- ▶ DO – focus on making decisions and reaching agreements – not just talking.

'People who would never think of committing suicide or ending their lives would think nothing of dribbling their lives away in useless minutes and hours everyday.'

THOMAS CARLYLE

52 Can you pass the measles test?

To find out how effective you are at handling paper, try this:

For the next week, every time you handle a piece of paper, mark it with a big red dot. If by the end of the week most of your pages have suffered an outbreak of measles, try this:

RAFT

First, face up to paperwork – look at every piece of paper on your desk. Then either **R**efer it (give it to someone else). **A**ct on it (then put it away). **F**ile it. Or **T**hrow it.

'Try not to become a man of success but rather try to become a man of value.'

EINSTEIN

71

People management

Four

53 Trust

Trust is one of the most important values in a progressive company. Without trust your business may never be outstanding. A lack of trust can be discerned if managers watch their people too closely. This can only result in poor performance. Instead of this, managers should train and trust their people, giving them the freedom and authority to make decisions and take risks without the fear of punishment for mistakes.

'Empowerment' has become a buzzword in management, however what managers should really be talking about is trust. If you don't trust your staff to do whatever it is they are employed to do, then it can only be for one of three reasons:

► They are the wrong people

► They haven't been given the training or guidance in advance

► You keep getting in their way.

So next time – probably very soon – when one of your people comes to you with some problem or other – send them out with this instruction: 'I trust you to decide the best course of action – let me know how you get on. If you need me to do anything, or if there is anything you need to ask, just let me know'.

'When the best leader's work is done her or his people say "We did it ourselves".'

54 Create champions of change

Organisations are often inert and difficult. It is a management problem, not a corporate sized problem. As soon as you get more than about 50 people in a business it needs a structure; as soon as you get over 150 people you have a living monster that has more in common with a business ten times that number.

People become managers of departments, resources and people. Their objectives are just that – theirs. Everybody starts to build their camp and throw flaming arrows into other peoples' camps.

To get over this, some companies have a 'champion' system to get new ideas through the layers of inertia. One person is given responsibility for championing an idea or a new product and he or she is offered a real (usually financial) stake in its success. The result is often electrifying. Innovation replaces inertia; creativity ceases to be crushed and even the timeservers start thinking of new ideas.

Need convincing? For over twenty years IBM struggled to know what to do with a loss-making printer division that didn't fit into any product strategy and was therefore deprived of investment and attention. Lexmark printers was formed by the management and staff of that very same division, which, when freed from its bureaucratic and corporate shackles, was transformed into a leading force in less than a year.

Demand that staff come up with ideas. Creativity, freethinking and anarchistic suggestions should become mandatory. Then whenever somebody has that 'look' in their eyes that tells you they are on to something, let them champion long enough to test it out. Think of it as the intellectual equivalent of drilling oil wells.

'After all, nobody was ever fired for the bold move they didn't make. But boldness is vital these days!'

55 How to make people twice as good at their jobs

It's easy; believe that people are twice as good at their jobs and quite soon you'll find that you were right.

Almost all the people in almost every company, in almost every country in the world, are capable of almost twice their current achievements. Don't believe it? It might be you who is holding your company back.

Try this. Accept the following maxim as gospel for a week: 'It is impossible to motivate people – only to demotivate them!' Yes, that's right – they motivate themselves – if you get out of their way. Consider how much they might achieve in their family and leisure time, only to do the minimum when they come to work.

Puzzled at what you do that demotivates them? Why not try asking them. Alternatively make a list of what demotivates you, either now or in the past. Chances are it's the same.

Create a motivating environment, give people encouragement, and a chance to prove what they can do and stop aggravating them.

77

'Most of your employees are keen, smart, quick-witted, motivated, enthusiastic and hard-working, except for the eight hours a day they work for you.'

56 Management by walking about

Radical times call for radical management. It calls for a new style – consultative not commanding; listening not directing; seeking information not controlling. Admit that you don't know everything and that you don't have all the answers. Take time to converse proactively and frequently with those who do – your customers, staff and suppliers.

Remember, listening is not just politely keeping quiet long enough for you to think of your next sentence.

For a start, move out of your office into the same open-plan environment as your staff, better still get rid of your desk.

Some of the world's most successful managers have neither offices nor secretaries. Instead, they believe their job is simply to walk around the organisation encouraging, motivating and helping the people who really run it, to run it really well. What happens when they need to write to someone or reply to mail? They don't! Nobody writes to them, they've delegated everything!

"My door is always open" has to be the second biggest lie in management. "People are our greatest resource is the first".

57 Set quarterly budgets – not annual

Have you noticed how budget panic usually happens most in the second half of the year? In the first half, even if things are going badly you think, 'Oh well, never mind, we can always make it up in the second half'. So how about forgetting annual budgets altogether and replacing them with quarterly budgets. This way you panic all the time, but you're more accurate and achieve a lot more!

Why waste all that management and planning time during the annual budget 'round', only to have to revise them all just a few short weeks later.

Nobody, whether they are sales people, chief executives, consultants or governments can truly predict the business drivers, dynamics and environment in twelve months time, let alone six – so why try?

Instead, empower managers by having them truly understand the goals of your organisation and devise their requirements and forecasts with more sensible, practical and realistic budgets.

79

'A budget is just a device for worrying about money before you've spent it.'

58 Develop an employee attrition programme

Yes, I know what you're thinking. Didn't this book just say to develop a policy to keep my staff, and now it's telling me to lose them! Which is it? Actually both.

In today's global economic world companies operate under different rules of employment than the previous generation, and even the previous decade. Here are the facts:

▶ Companies will shift production or offices to low-cost or low wage countries or regions, regardless of whether they are making a loss or a profit. Short-term, cost-saving, profit-boosting management does not wait for economy downturns to make changes. Today's employees and managers have equal levels of job insecurity, whether they work for a successful company or a loss-making one.

▶ If you could fire 80 per cent of your non-specialist staff and hire them for 20 per cent less you would, or rather you would if you didn't have to look them in the eye when you did it. The facts are Jill and John in accounts, or personnel or wherever are the modern equivalent of mill-workers. They are hired hands not necessarily hired brains. They may well have been with you for 20 years, and have received regular RPI wage increases every year. There is a good chance that their job could be done as well, if not better, by someone younger, without a family to support and prepared to work for a lower wage.

▶ You cannot offer your staff long-term careers, or even long-term jobs, and most of the smart ones know this. It is irresponsible to let them believe otherwise.

▶ Therefore, the reality of this is that the only way most of us can jump our salary and responsibilities is to increase our value and net worth to an enterprise.

59 ACHIEVE – Performance review method

If your staff performance review is not a thoughtful, consistent and fair one, then motivation, morale, and improved self-concept are all put in jeopardy. There are three parts to a good performance review system:

1 Performance planning
2 Day-to-day coaching
3 Performance evaluation.

Performance planning involves goals and objectives. A manager must agree clear and measurable goals with each and every staff member. All good performance starts here and leads to people feeling like winners.

Day-to-day coaching helps staff members win and is a necessary skill for successful managers. Day-to-day coaching means managing by values, or continually reinforcing why your company holds particular beliefs and practices; why it is doing what it is doing; and why you expect your staff members to do what you've asked them to.

The **ACHIEVE** model gives managers particular elements to use in day-to-day coaching to help their people perform:

A *Ability.* Does this person have the ability to do the job you're asking him or her to do?

C *Clarity.* Are the goals and objectives you've agreed with him or her stated as clearly as possible?

H *Help.* Are you going to give him or her the help needed to achieve the necessary ability and confidence to achieve the goal?

I *Incentive.* Does this person know what reward he or she will receive when the goal is accomplished?

E *Evaluate.* Has the way in which he or she will be evaluated been discussed and made clear?

V *Validity.* Does this person know why he or she has been chosen for a particular task or goal?

E *Environment.* Has an environment conducive to completing this job been provided?

Performance evaluation means sitting down and looking over a person's performance, individually and regularly. Issues such as honesty in your appraisal, open communication and supportive feedback, and the ability to motivate a staff member upward through his or her hierarchy of needs, have already been discussed.

It is important for managers to note that it is often useful for them to look at their staff members as children – in a non-patronising way. Like children, your staff members need praise, encouragement, patience, and clear goals. Use the performance evaluation to provide these essentials. Also use it as an evaluation of yourself as a manager. What kind of job have you done in giving your staff members what they need to reach their goals?

60
Adopt a 'buddy' principle

Do you remember your first day at school? Wouldn't it have been nice if another child who knew the ropes had befriended you, shown you where the toilets were and saved you a seat in the canteen? Starting a new job is almost as bad as starting a new school. People tend to be more effective, more quickly, if the same principle is applied.

Try assigning a 'buddy' or 'mentor' to every newcomer and you'll find they assimilate into the corporate culture in a fraction of the time it used to take.

'Do all the good you can,

By all the means you can,

In all the ways you can,

In all the places you can,

At all the times you can,

To all the people you can,

As long as ever you can.'

JOHN WESLEY

83

61 Organising your organisation – 1

There are about 100 theories on this alone, but here's an interesting one: never draw anything in ink.

Believe that leaders are created solely by the respect of those they lead and not by boxes and lines on pieces of paper. If you really have to sketch the structure of some part of your business, do it in pencil and have the eraser ready.

'Whatever you can do, or dream you can...
Begin it. For Boldness has Genius, Power and
Magic in it. Begin it NOW!'

GOETHE

62 Organising your organisation – 2

The result of all the constant changes in working practices is that organisations have become much flatter.

This is not simply a matter of removing layers of middle management through 'de-layering' or 'right sizing', which all too often become a cost cutting exercise as an end in itself. Rather, it is a conscious effort to focus on the customer, cutting out all those things that get in the way of that focus: bureaucracy, hierarchy, overheads and functionalism. As a result, the whole structure of the organisation is changed: 'Five years ago the corporate structure was like a pyramid with very steep sides, in fact one could say stalactites. Now it is more like a plate of peas'.

The number of levels in an organisation are cut to as few as possible. In some instances there are only three levels within the organisation: directors, managers and people. Seniority, and its rewards, no longer comes with length of service but rather as a result of merit, experience and knowledge.

If you must have a chart, try not to make it a hierarchy. Take your existing organisational chart (which is probably a pyramid with the boss at the top) and change its shape completely. Ask yourself 'who are the most important people to my organisation?' (if you answer anything but customers, you're wrong) and place them at the top. Next, put the people who are in contact with customers most often. Then, put the people who don't see the customers much but help the people who do. When you've gone through all the layers of reducing customer contact put the chairman at the bottom.

'More will be accomplished, and better, and with more ease, if every man does what he is best fitted to do, and nothing else.'

PLATO

63 Holidays

If you have the kind of organisation in which people feel they can't take their full holiday entitlement, you should immediately go on holiday and work out ways to change this. No one is irreplaceable, especially for only four or five weeks. Holidays are vital for your people's health and your organisation's welfare. Who wants a business full of tired, jaded dullards?

'Don't forget until it's too late that the business of life is not business, but living.'

B. C. FORBES

87

64 Where you can stick your stick

Some people believe that you should do more than try to equalise the praise/criticism ratio. They say that criticism is actually unnecessary. If someone does something wrong there will be three possible causes:

1 They don't know how to do it right

2 They know how to do it right, but they didn't know you wanted them to do it right

3 They know how to do it right, they know you want them to do it right, but a personal problem is getting in the way.

Criticism would have absolutely no effect in any of these situations. Instead, you should give training to solve situation 1. You should coach and explain your requirements to solve situation 2 and for situation 3, you should counsel the employee to uncover the problem, then help him or her to solve it.

65 Get more complaints

Establish a culture in which employees can air their grievances without
risk. It is hypocritical to encourage customer complaints, yet repress
ones from employees.

'*The tougher you are on yourself, the easier life will
be on you.*'

ZIG ZIGLAR

66 Responsibility

People become what they do. When you give your people more responsibilities and encourage their creativity, they became responsible, self-starting and creative. If you take responsibility for other people, they'll never take it for themselves.

'The only way to develop responsibility in people is to give them responsibility.'

67
Eliminate excuses

Create a culture where all excuses for poor service or poor job perform-ance are eliminated. Make each employee accountable for his/her own actions.

Instead of centralising customer responsibility into a department, make sure that people deliver to customers personally. For example, if somebody in a post room forgets to send out an urgent customer consignment, they should telephone the customer to let them know what has happened and what is being done about it. Do not allow people to pass the buck to customer services or blame the sales department, for example.

Where things need to be handled by different functions, create teams allocated to 'customer portfolios' so that people are accountable and have a clear sense of contribution. This will actually be more attrac-tive to most people, and will increase their job satisfaction.

68 What makes an extraordinary company?

Easy! Extraordinary people!

You don't need an extraordinary product to be extraordinary; all you need is a group of special people. How do you get them? You have them already!

What you see is what you get!

Here are some ways of helping to get extraordinary performance from your people:

► Delegate decision-making and stand well back!

► Push decisions down to the lowest levels
Many outstanding managers believe that it is important to push decisions as far 'down' as possible. They empower people so that decisions are made by those closest to the people affected by them. The result is high performing, highly committed employees, including assembly line workers, reception staff and salespeople.

► Make change the constant

► How to welcome change
The key to welcoming change is to make sure you're never surprised by it. You do this by staying informed. This means keeping abreast of changes in your field, as well as being knowledgeable about as many other things as possible. It means being well read, keeping in touch with world events and embracing new technology.

► Incompetent until proven otherwise
In non-outstanding businesses employees are considered incompetent until proven otherwise. Managers and supervisors watch so closely that employees have a built-in excuse for not producing quality. People need space to give their best performance.

▶ Setting objectives
Set objectives for your employees in a consultative rather than a dictatorial way. People are more likely to reach their goals when they help to define them.

▶ Be eager to praise
If you wait until you get perfection before you reward people, you'll never get exceptional results. Praise the small victories on the road to high performance. Find three things to say a sincere 'thank you' for everyday. If you can't find three, does it mean that nobody has done anything worthy of the comment, that you have noticed, or taken the time to notice?

'Nothing in the world can take the place of persistence.

Talent will not: nothing is more common than unsuccessful men with talent are.

Genius will not: unrewarded genius is almost a proverb.

Education will not: the world is full of educated derelicts.

Persistence and determination alone are omnipotent.

The slogan 'press on' has solved and always will solve the problems of the human race.'

PRESIDENT CALVIN COOLIDGE

93

69 Free PR

If you don't value your employees, you can't expect them to value your customers. The benefits of treating people well are remarkable. They stay longer, work better and repeatedly cause a most unusual phenomenon – the delighted customer.

'*Employees are the best PR – invest in them as you would an award-winning advertising campaign.*'

70 Delegation, empowerment and unemployment

Everyone knows that managers are supposed to delegate ruthlessly and empower their people fearlessly, but very few people actually do it because the ultimate effect could be to eliminate the manager's role!

When you think about it though, isn't this a great idea?

Such an effective manager would be in great demand everywhere as so few people genuinely delegate and empower. By definition, he or she would change companies quite often, but the salary hike each time would probably make up for the inconvenience.

95

'Delegation is simply the application of the equation $1+1=3$.'

71

How to get paid for having fun

It's easy. Make your job fun – as in enjoyable or refreshing.

You owe it to yourself and to your staff to make your organisation the kind of place people want to go to on Monday mornings.

How? Well, if you have any rules about clothing, workspace, decoration, office sizes, carpet sizes, desk types or parking spaces, rewrite them.

▶ Make Friday a jeans day

▶ Get a karaoke machine in every Wednesday lunchtime

▶ Get a table magician in on Mondays

▶ Get the IT department to completely change all the on-screen messages for your computer system, especially the one that says 'please wait'. It should now say 'Why not get yourself a cup of coffee, I'll be with you as soon as I can'

▶ Give everyone nicknames

▶ Give spot prizes for innovation

▶ Host family picnics and out-of-hours sports competitions

▶ Start meetings with jokes, tongue twisters or ice breakers.

Don't try and decide what will make your workplace fun – just look for opportunities for more enjoyment and encourage everybody else to do the same.

'If you're not in business for profit or fun, get out now.'

97

72 Act as if you own the company

Whenever you're faced with a decision to make, ask yourself: 'What would I do if it were my company?' and do just that. If it's already your own company, be sure not to criticise your people if they start acting like the owner. It means they have finally taken the initiative you have been omitting to give them.

Encourage everybody to think and act like a shareholder. Better still, make them shareholders. Have you noticed the difference in attitude and activity between self-employed and employed people. To generalise, probably unfairly, the former group do the most they can, the other, the least they can get away with. It has been suggested that big companies employ staff that are least likely to fail, and small ones employ staff that are most likely to succeed. Which group do you fall into?

73 Recruitment and the imperfect person

Have you ever looked for that 'perfect' human being when recruiting?

For example: the one with the best school, college and university results and an uninterrupted career path? The one who was school prefect, head of the debating society, and is now leader of the local 'Neighbourhood Watch'. What about deliberately setting out to find the most important, unusual, quirky, interesting applicants and giving them the next few jobs. In an unusual, quirky and interesting business world, it might just be the breath of fresh air that your company needs.

'Five per cent of the people think, ten per cent of the people think they think; and the other eighty-five per cent would rather die than think.'

ANON

99

74 Company policy

Some companies have vast policy manuals in which every possible contingency is covered, so that the company is protected both logistically and legally. But if their people are that inept, the company is either hiring the wrong people or not giving them enough training, or both. A company should never have to protect itself from its customers and employees.

75 Team meetings

Meetings have a very important place to play in building a successful team. Properly run they can give recognition to achievers and motivation to those trying to progress.

They can make everyone feel part of the team, which is vital, particularly if your people are front line staff based away from the office. They are also vital for communicating new policies, products and procedures, and if time allows, can also be used for planning and generating new ideas.

How often you choose to run them is dependent on your own preference and how easy it is for the team to get together. The rule is the more regularly they are held, the shorter they should be; ranging from perhaps twenty to thirty minutes for a daily meeting to a full day for a quarterly conference.

▶ Run team meetings once a week for each department or group of eight or so people, e.g. sales, customer service, etc

▶ Make them interesting and enjoyable

▶ Set a time limit on the meeting, set a punchy agenda, and stick to it

▶ Include some brainstorming sessions and involve people in finding ideas for improving your processes and customer service

▶ Show a training video or give a short training session on some aspect of the business

101

- ▶ Invite someone from another area to give a talk on how they work in the company
- ▶ Ask each person to give a brief (one or two minutes) on their week's activity and results
- ▶ Run a quick quiz to keep everybody on their toes
- ▶ Make sure the meeting is positive and to the point, avoid long discussions on things you can't easily change or influence
- ▶ Ask people to research and prepare presentations on set topics, such as your competitors, customer complaints etc
- ▶ Vary the time that you hold them, people are more alert and keen to contribute on a Monday morning than last thing on a Friday afternoon.

'The two most important elements in building a team are proximity and a common enemy.'

76 Let people appraise themselves

Let's face it; nobody enjoys the annual or biannual appraisal. Managers find them embarrassing, time consuming and of little practical value, and staff hate them. They also have little connection with performance pay or bonuses. The best alternative by far is to let people appraise themselves.

77 The 50 per cent rule

Here's a recruitment principle that can also transform morale and team-sprit throughout an organisation. When promoting people, don't look outside, or for someone in the organisation who can do the job, look for someone in the organisation who can do 50 per cent of the job. Why? Because people always grow when you let them.

78 Nothing impresses like competence

Make sure that everybody in your organisation does everything they do to the best of their ability. Instill a feeling of pride into every single job in the company; be it making a sale, typing a letter or cleaning the floor.

Before you start using any particular tricks, techniques, promotions or special devices to keep your customers, 'your customers', there is one inescapable fact: nothing impresses a customer like competence.

Customers go back to businesses that they like and that do things right, first time, every time. They go back to businesses that they enjoy dealing with, they enjoy people who are nice to them and they enjoy people who work hard to keep them satisfied. This is not a particularly difficult idea, in fact it should seem just like common sense.

However, the paradox is that common sense is not common practice. As Vince Lombardi, the great American football coach once remarked, '…let's become brilliant on the basics'.

105

'There always seems to be enough time to do things right the second time.'

79 Lead by vision and values, not commands

White water change

There are a lot of changes going on in business today. From layoffs and downsizing to mergers and acquisitions, the face of business has changed and is changing. Unlike changes in the past, today's changes are not stabilising into a period of relative calm, but instead they seem to be layered one on top of another in successive initiatives that all seem to be pursued concurrently. Think of it as white water change.

White water change places new demands on effective managers who are interested in getting the best results from their employees. It is increasingly difficult to accurately tell people what the best thing is that they should be doing to be most effective in their jobs. This is because their jobs, and their working environment, are changing to tap into the energy, ideas and initiative on the part of each employee in your work group.

'People who say something can't be done are usually interrupted by those doing it!'

ANON

80 Involve people in order to commit them

Involvement equals commitment. To garner the commitment and enthusiasm for individual employees to do their best, you need to start with a level of trust and respect that says: 'We're in it together'. How employees are treated during stressful times of change will say a lot about how they are truly regarded by management. Are they pawns in a game to be played with or individuals to be treated with respect? No matter what the change is, there is a humane way to make it, and that is typically the best way.

Management today is what you do with people, not what you do to them. In order to get the most from your people, you need to start with them: who they are, what they want, what they need, and then build upon that foundation by putting the best interests of your employees first. Doing so will allow you to obtain a multi-fold payback in results as employees strive to do the best job they can for you and the organisation.

81 Communicate more, not less

As a basic lubricant in keeping today's organisations running smoothly, there is perhaps none better than communication. During times of turbulence, you need to increase the quality and quantity of your communication. Part of this is because there is greater distortion in a quickly changing system, that is, the lines of communication that have served you well in the past, may not work well today. Older communication channels may be overloaded, too formal or too slow to get employees information when they most need it.

Instead, experiment with new ways of getting the important messages across:

► Informal sessions with top managers

► Message boards

► Electronic displays for progress toward organisational goals

► Chat sessions on the intranet/internet

► Hotlines for employee questions and concerns.

Some will work, some will not, but by constantly innovating, you will be trying to meet employees on their own turf, and they will respect and continue to serve you well in return.

82 Rewarding yourself

The best managers today tend to be employee-focused, looking to help others succeed in their jobs.

They know the power of positive reinforcement, that is, catching other people doing something right, in working with others and recognising and rewarding them for their efforts and results. These managers know that by providing a positive consequence, whether it is a word of thanks, taking someone out to lunch, or creating a special award, they greatly increase the chances of having the desired behaviour repeated or the high performance even further enhanced. They know the greatest management principle in the world is: 'You get what you reward'.

How often, however, do you, as a manager, take time to reward yourself? Even though you may be extremely busy, as most managers are today, it's important to take time out for yourself. To relax, and give yourself a chance to regenerate is essential to remain fresh and effective, whatever your position is.

Taking a break from your routine helps to stimulate your thinking as well. Jack Canfield, co-author of *Chicken Soup for the Soul*, advises others to '…increase the amount of time you get away from the office so you can increase the high-level thinking required to come up with big ideas. When I come back to work (from vacation), I immediately see the results. I'm more productive and creative. While on vacation, I'll also get incredible ideas that wouldn't happen at home because I'm too busy putting out fires'.

Jack also gets energy by spending time with others. He belongs to a Master Mind group, a term coined by legendary motivational guru, Napoleon Hill, author of *Think and Grow Rich*, who suggested people

109

form support groups to motivate and inspire each other. Jack says, 'We all get locked into our own myopic viewpoints and very rarely get to see other, broader points of view. Regular meetings with successful people from different professions helps open our thinking to new, bigger possibilities'.

What works best to relax and rejuvenate of course varies widely from person to person, so it is important to be aware of what things you find most satisfying and rewarding. For some people, it is reading; for others, it may be exercise; still others might like to buy something for themselves during a stressful time to acknowledge a milestone, or as a way of picking up their spirits when they feel down.

83 Creative recruitment

Finding good people is getting harder, finding the right people is harder still. Here is a collection of ideas that might help you to achieve these goals:

▶ Start a bounty programme. That is, offer a payment to existing staff if they refer people to the organisation for vacancies. Make this payment big, not just a token gesture. It should be equal to what you might expect to spend on other measures – advertising, recruitment companies, etc

▶ Interview at least three people for each position

▶ See each shortlisted candidate three times

▶ Have at least three people offer an opinion before offering a new person a position

▶ Conduct a tough interview – try and catch a glimpse of the real person – not just the polished and prepared interview technique

▶ Make the interview practical – doing things, giving a presentation, role-play, problem solving, etc

▶ Interview telephone staff over the telephone.

When interviewing, pay attention to the following: How the applicant was dressed, how they sat, did they maintain good eye contact, personal grooming, sincerity, manners, were they outgoing, shy or loud and noisy?

▶ Do they have that 'gleam-in-the-eye' that tells you they want the opportunity to perform rather than 'just a job for the income they need'. Are you sure it is a 'gleam in the eye' or is it more of a 'burned-out' look?

▶ Will this person fit in well with fellow employees and is this person a significant cut above the person who had this job previously?

▶ Use and trust your 'gut-reaction'. If something is 'just not right' about the person, even if you can't put your finger on it, better to pass them up. However, don't confuse the above with someone who doesn't fit your personal lifestyle (neat, ordered, choice of music, etc) when making this decision.

84 Creative questions for interviews

The following questions are obviously designed to let you find out as much meaningful information about a prospective employee as possible, before you make your final choice.

You might want to circle certain questions that apply more to the position you are trying to fill. Asking questions that would apply to a salesman would not be very meaningful for a maintenance engineer. You might want to design your own set of questions for different kinds of jobs.

You should make your own notes and comments as to what would be the best and worst answers to each of the questions you intend to ask. You may have to probe a bit to get to the meat of the answer, but be careful not to lead the applicant to the answer you want to hear. Talk as little as possible and listen a lot. Do not fill in the silent periods too quickly since some of the best answers will come after this time. Encourage the applicant to talk freely and try not to write very much. After they have left, make extensive notes around each question while the interview is fresh in your mind.

Interview questions

1   Tell me about yourself...your background... your interests in life, in the past as well as now.

2   What do you do for recreation and entertainment off the job?

3   What kind of books and magazines do you read? (Probe for many answers – this will tell you about personal interests.)

4   What was the thing you liked best about your last job?

5   What was the thing you liked least about your last job?

6   Think of something you have accomplished in your life that you are especially proud of.... What was it and how did you go about accomplishing that thing?

7 Does it bother you to make a mistake? How do you feel about mistakes? What is your feeling when others make a mistake? How about when others make a lot of mistakes?

8 What do you know about this company and this job that interests you?

9 What is it about yourself that makes you believe you could do a good and effective job in the position we are discussing?

10 Why did you leave your last two jobs? What would your immediate supervisor say about you and your work at those two companies?

11 Are you currently involved in any clubs or community activities? Please tell me about them. (Too much or too little might be a problem area. You can also discover what is important in this person's life and what motivates him/her to do things that he/she doesn't have to do.)

12 If you were to leave your present job, how long would it take to replace you? Why? (Does this person keep all-important work to themselves and not delegate or build support people? The 'loner', good as they are, may not be what you are looking for. On the other hand, a 'loner' who will have to accomplish much virtually on their own in an isolated environment, may be just what you were looking for.)

13 What is the single hardest job you've ever had to do? How did you do it?

14 If you are working with another employee and you are doing the bulk of the work and they are 'goofing-off' but still getting half the credit, how would you handle it? What would you do about it?

15 How do you handle criticism? (Probe, don't settle for the short, quick answer like, 'I welcome it'. We are not looking for someone who ignores it, nor are we likely to want someone who seems to like regular abuse with whips and chains either.)

16 How do you feel about emotional outbursts on the job? When others do it, do you feel sympathy, anger, or ignore it?

17 (**VERY IMPORTANT**) What questions do you have about this company, the job in particular, company policies, benefits, and opportunities? (Look for questions about advancement policies, latitude to try new things, ideas and freedom to grow; instead of questions about retirement, holiday policies, sick leave, insurance and other pure benefits.)

18 If you don't get this job, how will you feel? (This question can tell you a lot about the applicant's personality if you know how to read between the lines of what they say. Do they cover real feelings? Do they try to impress you with their answer? What's really going on as they reply to this one?)

19 What else can you tell me that would further your chances in getting hired for this position with this company? (This is a catch-all, but probe for personal qualities and attitude since they are more likely to respond with training and experience in past jobs.)

85 Starting off new team members

If people are your most important (and probably most expensive) asset then it is vital that you start them off on the right track when they join your company, department or team. Here is a simple, and proven, action plan:

1   Clarify the organisation's goals and your expectations regarding hours, resources, performance and results.

2   Be sure the newcomer understands the importance of becoming accepted initially and building teamwork continuously.

3   Reintroduce the newcomer to people who were met during the employment screening process, and include introductions to others with whom interaction is likely.

4   Provide a clear understanding of policies, procedures (formal or informal), codes of conduct, and standards of ethics that will be expected for the person to function properly.

5   Discuss such basics as the organisation's structure, the company's physical facilities, locations of toilets, and lunch or break areas, and their use.

6   Review the manner in which the employee will be paid, overtime rules, bonus or incentive plans, elements of the benefit package and payroll deduction items.

7   Whenever possible, support your comments with copies of employee handbooks, policy and procedure manuals, a letter or memo welcoming your associate, and other useful background or reference documents.

8   Check more frequently than you might think necessary regarding any questions or requests for help that the newcomer may have.

9   Take every legitimate opportunity to reinforce early progress on either task or relationship matters as you observe or hear of things being done well.

10 Above all, take the time to handle these steps well. You are making a sound investment, not just for the individual, but for the team!

Motivation

Five

86 Understanding what motivates people

One of a manager's main jobs is to increase the return on his or her investment in people; to get better and higher performance from them. This is done through motivation.

But what motivates people? What causes some people to perform consistently at ever-higher levels, when others do the bare minimum necessary to keep themselves from being fired? There are as many motivating factors as there are individuals in your workplace.

The manager as motivator

The fact is that you cannot motive people directly, you can only demotivate them. However, you can create an environment that will allow them to motivate themselves.

People do things for reasons, these are called motives. Everything an employee does is to satisfy a motive. If an employee fails to do something, it is generally because he or she does not see any personal advantage in doing it, it does not satisfy some motive.

Your job is to understand the psychological and motivational 'hot-buttons' of all your people and apply Maslow's hierarchy of needs.

Maslow's work is the standard for discussion on what human beings want out of life. Maslow's hierarchy of needs states that there is an ascending order of needs we seek to fulfil, from the most basic to the uniquely personal. At each level there are needs that must be met prior to moving to the next level and its corresponding needs.

The lowest level of needs in Maslow's hierarchy are physiological; the essentials required for simply staying alive:

▶ Food
▶ Water
▶ Shelter.

Once these physiological needs are met, we concern ourselves with safety and security needs:

▶ Freedom from physical harm

▶ A continuing, dependable income.

Following safety and security needs are more sophisticated social needs:

▶ Belonging to a group, either family, friends, or at work

▶ Boosts to your self-esteem.

And at the highest level is self-actualisation:

▶ Doing something interesting and fulfilling

▶ Being the best you can be

▶ Enjoying the coming together of all parts of your life.

The one factor that is the key to all levels of Maslow's hierarchy is employment:

▶ At the physiological level, a job pays for shelter and food

▶ At the safety and security level, employment provides needed income, but sometimes raises questions of physical safety, as well as loyalty concerns

▶ At the social level, a job provides an opportunity to work with others, to join in with decision-making, and to receive praise and promotions

▶ At the self-actualisation level, it is through a profession or career that most people are able to become the very best they can be, to pull together all aspects of themselves to create a satisfying pattern of achievement; even more than money – though that, too, is powerful – a challenging, interesting, fulfilling job is a prime motivator toward self-actualisation.

Summary – Maslow's ladder of motivation in work

Self-actualisation
Set standards of peak performance, training, coaching, implementing ideas, and encourage excellence.

Recognition
Prizes, awards, celebrations, charts, graphs, delegating, involvement, one-to-one time, sincere compliments.

Acceptance
Socialising, team meetings, group events, casual encouragement, friendliness, personal regard.

Security
Reassurance, big picture, casual encouragement, friendliness, personal regard, job content, open communication.

Survival
Encouragement, salary, commission, consistent decision-making, honesty, fairness.

'You can make more friends in two months by becoming really interested in other people than you can in two years by trying to get other people interested in you.'

DALE CARNEGIE

87

Motivation is personal

Every person is different. A manager's job is to get people to do things because they want to do them. The successful manager is one who provides his or her employees with the opportunity to satisfy their own needs. They will work because they see that by doing so they will satisfy their individual needs. Before a manager can provide this opportunity, he or she must be aware of the things that motivate their employees.

Matching jobs and individual needs is one way to satisfy employees' needs. If an employee is placed in a position that is challenging and satisfies his or her needs, motivation will not be a problem.

This may mean reworking jobs to make them more complex, more challenging, and hopefully, more satisfying to the employee. Matching employee needs with jobs is a very difficult process.

Once the manager understands what an employee's basic needs are, he or she can be more sensitive to these needs and try to match the employee with jobs that offer him or her the opportunity to satisfy individual needs.

Whatever motivates you most is what you believe motivates everybody else as well. Many surveys show that managers do not really understand what workers want out of their jobs.

121

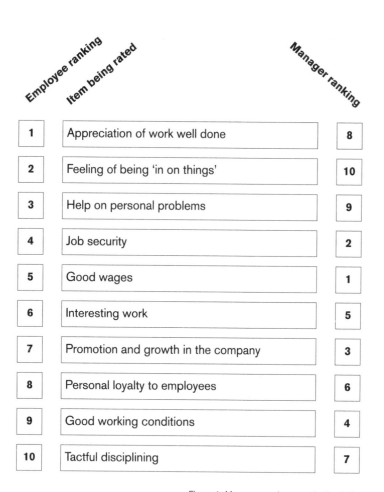

Employee ranking	Item being rated	Manager ranking
1	Appreciation of work well done	8
2	Feeling of being 'in on things'	10
3	Help on personal problems	9
4	Job security	2
5	Good wages	1
6	Interesting work	5
7	Promotion and growth in the company	3
8	Personal loyalty to employees	6
9	Good working conditions	4
10	Tactful disciplining	7

Figure 1: Manager-employee motivation index

This research does not prove that money, good working conditions, and loyalty to employees are relatively unimportant. These factors are extremely important and companies need to continually strive to be competitive in these areas. All ten factors are important needs to all employees. Most employees expect a company to provide good working conditions, fair pay, an opportunity for growth, and interesting work.

Most companies attempt to provide these. Lower ranked needs are very important and if they are not satisfied, employees will be less motivated to achieve higher needs. What is important to notice from the research is that the needs that are most important to most employees are social and esteem needs, therefore close attention should be paid to these areas.

'We act as though comfort and luxury are the chief requirements of life, when all that we need to make us really happy is something to be enthusiastic about.'

123

88 Daily motivational strategies

The following strategies are useful in meeting the social and esteem needs of team members:

1 Treat team members as individuals
2 Be sincere with praise
3 Promote participation
4 Make the work interesting
5 Promote cooperation and teamwork
6 Provide growth opportunities.

There is no magic formula for motivating team members. Perhaps the best approach for getting team members to work along with you is to remember the following:

1 Communicate with people frequently and praise them
2 Consult with people about their work
3 Encourage people to participate in setting goals on the job
4 Counsel people about teamwork and opportunities etc.

'If you would hit the mark, you must aim a little above it: Every arrow that flies feels the attraction of the earth.'

LONGFELLOW

89 Ms or Mr Motivator

What are the characteristics of the manager who most successfully motivates his or her team members? He or she is not the 'cheerleader' type, or the one who uses fear. Neither do they play their cards 'close to their chest' or make all of the decisions themselves.

If you want to be the kind of manager who motivates his or her team members best, then do the following:

▶ Establish and review realistic goals for yourself and others – goals that are worthwhile, challenging and attainable.

▶ Make decisions after relevant participation by your subordinates. Seek their thoughts and be seriously interested in their ideas.

▶ Seek and give feedback to your team members about how they are doing, the progress they are making, and the problems that are coming up. Because of your open communication and feedback, your team members will be motivated to perform well. They will openly evaluate their progress, and they will not hesitate to seek changes when they think they are needed.

▶ Resolve conflicts with good judgement, understanding, and openness. Focus on solving the conflict rather than placing blame. Attempt to understand the problem and find the best solution.

▶ Always communicate to your team members, explaining what is being done and why. Talk honestly and openly about how you feel about things. This process of open and continuous communication lets the team members know what is going on inside you.

▶ Always listen to what your team members tell you, try to understand what they are saying, and make good comments about their ideas. Don't hesitate to question them and ask them, 'How about explaining that again to me?'. Being listened to makes the employee feel important and also makes him or her more willing to listen to what the boss says.

▶ Be genuinely interested in your team members as individuals. Be interested in their growth and future progress.

▶ Be open and sincere in praise, reprimand in private and praise in public.

▶ Control your temper. When angry, managers should not brood. They should approach the employee directly and express their feelings honestly. This encourages dialogue between manager and employee and a major crisis can be disposed of as a minor problem.

▶ You must be open-minded, always willing to listen to new ideas – even those that are different from your own. You shouldn't mind criticism, and you should readily admit to your mistakes. You should be the type of person the employee would like to have as a personal friend.

▶ Use reprimands only when necessary and even then deliver them in private. Use them to educate and correct and not to punish an employee.

▶ Make jobs as interesting and desirable as possible.

▶ Don't be afraid to delegate and willingly give credit to your team members for a job well done.

▶ Don't try to get work out of your team members by threatening them.

▶ Don't be afraid to admit you are wrong and your team members are right.

▶ Actively seek the opportunity to promote your team members – even if it means losing them.

▶ Try to run an orderly department, bringing system to an otherwise confused situation.

▶ Be big enough not to compete with your team members for credit. Let team members bask in the spotlight for a job well done.

▶ Don't be condescending.

▶ Don't be a know-it-all.

What a motivational manager does:

▶ Focuses on vision

▶ Is proactive

▶ Promotes involvement

▶ Seeks excellence

▶ Facilitates

▶ Communicates

▶ Mediates conflict

▶ Quickly recognises achievements

▶ Keeps commitments.

90 Unlock the potential of your people

Motivated staff will be ten times more productive than unmotivated staff.

Creating a culture in which employees are genuinely empowered and focused on the customer is one of the key elements of the culture of winning companies.

The framework that makes innovation a habit in the company is where the people in the organisation are seen as a key resource rather than simply as a cost – the competition may copy the product but it cannot copy the people.

One of the main tasks of the winning manager is to enable each person in the organisation to fulfil his or her full potential through empowerment of that individual, whilst maintaining focus on the customer at all times.

There is a clear recognition that when a customer meets an employee they meet the whole organisation and often judge the whole company on that basis. Employees are encouraged to work with customers as key partners.

Invest in people through good training, teaming and communications. Training is seen as a key component in achieving empowerment of the individual and in maintaining focus on the customer in order to remain competitive. Not only is training the epicentre of empowerment, with as much as 10 per cent of employees' time spent on it, but successful companies use education as a competitive weapon. The aim is to provide employees with the necessary skills to allow them to meet the multiple challenges of the tasks facing them in order to satisfy the customer. However, training is not merely an end in itself: 'Everything is goal oriented; everything is measured with charts and score cards everywhere. Our practice is to set targets, empower the team and measure delivery'. All this is done where 'the customer is the focal point'.

Continuous communication forms an essential part of the process of empowerment and continuous change. Communication takes place in many directions throughout the organisation, and is always a two-way process. Just as the leaders of a company communicate their vision of where the company is going, they welcome and encourage feedback and ideas from all their employees for they recognise that all have something to offer: 'One proposal from each of our 100 employees is better than 100 proposals from one super boss'. Communication takes the form of regular team briefings, frequent internal newsletters and regular contacts with customers. In addition, senior management frequently gets out to meet employees by walking around the organisation and talking with individuals, encouraging the team concept of 'us' rather than the divisive 'them' and 'us'.

'"Quit now, you'll never make it."
If you disregard this advice you'll be halfway there.'

DAVID ZUCKER

91 How to win friends and influence people

The title above is a book by Dale Carnegie, which describes how influence and motivation go hand in hand. Listed below are the chapters in the book. For more insight, read the book. If you have read the book already, re-read it, the chances are that there are ideas that you have missed or forgotten.

1   Don't criticise, condemn or complain

2   Give honest, sincere appreciation

3   Arouse in the other person an eager want

4   Become genuinely interested in other people

5   Smile

6   Remember that a person's name is to that person the sweetest and most important sound

7   Be a good listener

8   Talk in terms of the other person's interest

9   Make the other person feel important and do it sincerely

10   The only way to get the best of an argument is to avoid it

11   Show respect for the other person's opinion and never say, 'you're wrong'

12   If you are wrong, admit it quickly and emphatically

13   Begin in a friendly way

14   Get the other person saying 'yes', 'yes' immediately

15   Let the other person do a great deal of the talking

16   Let the other person feel that the idea is his or hers

17 Try honestly to see things from the other person's point of view

18 Be sympathetic with the other person's ideas and desires

19 Appeal to the nobler motives

20 Dramatise your ideas

21 Throw down a challenge.

92 Simple gestures count the most

One of the best-kept secrets in management today is the power of recognising employees. Study after study has demonstrated that what employees want most is to be acknowledged for the jobs they do, day in and day out. This recognition does not have to be anything fancy, in fact, the simpler and more direct the better.

One of the most motivating forms of recognition, as reported by employees, is very simple indeed: taking the time to personally thank an employee for something they did well. This seems very obvious, yet when was the last time you did it? If you are typical, it has been some time. Have you taken the time to personally thank all your employees? Everyone needs to be appreciated – even those who are shy or more withdrawn.

To be most effective, your praise should come as soon as possible after the achievement or desired behaviour has occurred. If you wait too long to acknowledge a person, the gesture will loose its significance. Implicitly, the employee will figure that other things are more important to you than taking a few minutes with him or her.

You also need to be very specific about what you are praising the person for and why. Praise that is too general tends to seem insincere. But saying, 'Thanks for staying late to finish those calculations I needed. It was critical for my meeting this morning and I really appreciate your work', specifically says what and why an employee's effort was of value.

93 Carrots v sticks

The most widely used management tool in the history of human endeavour has been criticism. In terms of time spent doing it, it beats praise by about ten million to one. Maybe this is why we're all in so much trouble.

Why not try something radical tomorrow – start to turn the tables. Walk around your organisation and look for people who are doing something wrong, and ignore it for the moment. Do this benign walkabout for at least half an hour a day. By the end of the first week your entire department/organisation will feel different. Your people will be happier and you'll probably have forgotten all about those mistakes you spotted because there's so much good work going on. By the end of the first month, you should be noticing improved financial results and at the end of a year doing this, the effect will be so spectacular that you'll probably be headhunted by your biggest competitor.

133

'Talking is like playing the harp. There is as much in laying the hand on the strings to stop their vibrations, as in twanging them to bring out their music.'

OLIVER WENDELL HOLMES

94 Beware of 'employee of the month' programmes

Many companies use employee of the month awards. This may include a photograph with an engraved nameplate in the lobby of the business, perhaps a reserved parking place, an award and/or a small cash bonus.

As popular as these programmes are, they may not be the best for motivating today's employees. So what's wrong with them?

► It is difficult to motivate employees through a 'programme'. Programmes are often too distant and formal for individuals to get excited about.

► Motivation is very personal and stems primarily from the interaction between an employee and his or her manager.

► What is motivating to an individual also varies from person to person.

The best motivation comes from daily positive reinforcement by management of desired performance with as many employees as possible – not something that occurs once a month for a single employee.

When new, an employee of the month programme can stimulate much excitement, however, over time much of the thrill is often lost. Often the selection criteria for the programme isn't clear, and things such as 'Let's give it to someone in accounting – they never get it' or 'Sally can't get it – she already received it earlier this year', are overheard. In other instances, the programme reaches a saturation point where so many employees have received the award that it no longer seems special.

If you have to have an employee of the month programme, there are some things that can help it to be more successful:

1   Make sure other things are systematically being done to recognise employee performance in the workplace on a daily basis. Make sure, for example, that managers in your organisation know the importance of giving feedback on performance, timely praising, and informal recognition. This takes pressure off of the employee of the month programme as being your organisation's sole means for motivating employees.

2   Employee of the month programmes can be improved if nominations are open to everyone, not just certain groups of staff. This keeps the programme from being biased to favoured employees who have greater visibility.

3   A programme can be further improved if it is not limited to being given once a month, so as to seem like a quota, but is instead more closely tied to outstanding performance whenever that happens. This programme provides a method of recognising performance when it happens, not sometime later. It also allows daily performance to be 'rolled up' and celebrated once a month on a more formal basis.

4   For best results, strive to keep the programme fresh and flexible, and make changes in the programme as it begins to feel stale to targeted employees.

In summary, there are more effective ways to improve employee motivation, morale and initiative than are typically obtained from employee of the month programmes. But if used in conjunction with other techniques, and with an awareness of the potential pitfalls, employee of the month programmes still have a place in motivating today's employees.

95 Gainsharing

'Gainsharing' is for all employees

What is it? It is handing out cheques to each employee once a year when the company exceeds its profitability goals.

Gainsharing is a nice benefit to have, but like most financial corporate change programmes, it doesn't have much 'trophy value', that is, it doesn't create a lasting memory of the achievement or event.

To address that problem, perhaps create a fun event tied to the distribution of gainsharing cheques. After we had distributed cheques to all employees, we gave each employee an additional envelope of cash, whether it was £100 or £1,000 doesn't matter, on the condition that they went shopping and spent it on themselves within the next two hours. They then had to return to the company to show everyone what they had bought and why.

This can create a real fun and revealing experience. Most people enjoy shopping, especially when they are told to buy whatever they want to and not to come back with the change. In addition to giving employees a chance to buy something for themselves, we enhanced both morale and the level of team building that existed within the company. When everyone gets back together to share, the variety of purchases will be as varied as the employees themselves.

96 The power of 'I's

No cost job recognition that works

I'm convinced that the most important thing managers can do is to develop and maintain motivated employees. It has no cost, but rather is a function of the daily interactions that managers have with employees pertaining to work. Many of the no cost methods that can be most effective are also a part of most jobs. I remember some of the best from the first letter of the word, which I call 'the power of 'I's.'

Interesting work

At least part of everyone's job should be of high interest to them. As the management theorist, Frederick Herzberg once said, 'If you want someone to do a good job, give him or her a good job to do'. Some jobs may be inherently boring, but you can give anyone in such a job at least one task or project that's stimulating to that person. Name him or her to a suggestion committee that meets once a week, or to some other special group. The time away from the regular job is likely to be more than made up with increased productivity.

Information/communication/feedback

With presumed employment for life largely a thing of the past, employees want more than ever to know how they are doing in their jobs and how the company is doing in its business. Start telling them how the company makes money and how it spends money. Make sure there are ample channels of communication to encourage employees to be informed, ask questions and share information. At least some of the communication channels should directly involve management in non-intimidating circumstances. Soon, you'll have them turning out the lights when they're the last to leave a room.

137

Involvement/ownership in decisions

Involving employees, especially in decisions that affect them, is both respectful to them and practical. People that are closest to the problem or customer, typically have the best insight as to how a situation can be improved. They know what works and what doesn't, but often are never asked for their opinion. As you involve others, you increase their commitment and ease in implementing any new idea or change.

Independence/autonomy/flexibility

Most employees, especially experienced, top-performing employees, value being given room to do their job as they best see fit. All employees also appreciate having flexibility in their jobs. When you provide these factors to employees based on desired performance, it increases the likelihood that they will perform as desired, and bring additional initiative, ideas, and energy to the job as well.

Increased visibility/opportunity/responsibility

Everyone appreciates a manager who gives credit where credit is due. The chance to share the successes of employees with others throughout the organisation are almost limitless. In addition, most employee development is on-the-job development that comes from new learning opportunities and the chance to gain new skills and experience. Giving employees new opportunities to perform, learn, and grow as a form of recognition and thanks, is very motivating to most employees.

Beneath all of these techniques is a basic premise of trust and respect and having the best interests of your employees at heart. You will never get the best effort from your employees today by building a fire under them; rather, you need to find a way to build a fire within them to obtain extraordinary results from ordinary people.

97 ASAP-cubed: How to give effective praise

In building an outstanding organisation, praise is priceless, and it costs nothing. In one recent poll, workers named a personal praising from their manager for doing a good job as the number one most motivating corporate change programme; yet almost 60 per cent of employees say they seldom, if ever, receive such a praising from their manager.

Although giving effective praise seems like common sense, a lot of people have never learned how to do it.

Here is a useful acronym, ASAP-cubed, that can be used to remember the essential elements. That is, praise should be given as soon, as sincere, as specific, as personal, as positive, and as proactive as possible.

As soon

Timing is very important when using positive reinforcement, according to extensive research on the topic. You need to give others praise as soon as the achievement is complete or the desired behaviour is displayed. You might even interrupt someone who is in a meeting to provide a quick word of praise, until you are able to discuss the achievement with him or her at greater length.

As sincere

Words alone can fall flat if you are not sincere in why you are praising someone. You need to praise because you are truly appreciative and excited about the other person's success. Otherwise, it may come across as a manipulative tactic; something you are doing only when you want an employee to work late, for example.

As specific

Avoid generalities in favour of details of the achievement. 'You really turned that angry customer around – you let him unload all of his emotions and then focused on what you could do for him, not on what you could not do for him.'

As personal

A key to conveying your message is praising in person, face to face. This shows that the activity is important enough for you to put aside everything else you have to do and just focus on the other person. Since we all have limited time, those things we do personally indicate that they have a higher value to you.

As positive

Too many managers undercut praise with a concluding note of criticism. When you say something like, 'You did a great job on this report, but there were quite a few typos', the 'but' becomes a verbal erasure of all that came before. Save the corrective feedback for the next similar assignment.

As proactive

Lead with praising and 'catch people doing things right' or else you will tend to be reactive, typically about mistakes, in your interactions with others.

Self-development

Six

98
How to be the life and soul of your business

Have you ever wondered why some people are always the centre of attention? Often it's just natural charisma. But getting noticed is a skill that can be learnt. Practice stimulating attention from the outset. Be positive. In meetings or at any face to face encounter, know what you want before you speak.

'If you can't write your idea on the back of a business card, you don't have a clear idea.'

ANON

99 Let's take the helicopter view

Avoid meaningless phrases and repetitive language. Nothing is more likely to switch off another person's attention than old chestnuts like 'as a matter of fact', 'so to speak', 'at this moment in time', 'at the end of the day' and 'when all is said and done'. Everybody uses far too many 'fillers' like this. Monitor yourself and work on reducing their frequency.

Next time you are in a management or business meeting, especially if it involves any form of 'consultant', amuse yourself by playing 'jargon bingo'. Simply make a list of clichés, overused or empty expressions and cross them out whenever you hear them. Here are some to start you off:

▶ Paradigm

▶ On-going situation

▶ Interface with you

▶ Value added

▶ Low hanging fruit

▶ Outside the box

▶ Right-sizing

▶ Down-sizing

▶ Off-line discussion

▶ Window of opportunity

▶ Team-based unit

▶ Highly leveraged

▶ Resource deliverables

▶ Mission critical

▶ One on one time.

143

100 Ten keys to greater personal success

Do you believe it is possible to increase your results by application and your own efforts?

Obviously it is; the question is how? By working harder or smarter, being more creative or better planning?

Listed here are the key factors which will enable you to increase your personal productivity:

1 Look for the difference that makes the difference

An athlete wins a competition and receives two or three times the prize money and accolades of the second or third placed runners. Yet there were probably only a few hundredths of a second between the first few runners across the line. To an observer, their training methods and performance were very similar. The key to success is to look for the 'difference that makes the difference'.

2 Make your own luck

The second thing to increase results is to understand that there is no luck; there is only a long process of accumulation. Every overnight success is a result of many years of struggle and determination, of many smaller defeats and victories. As Gary Player once said, after potting a hole in one, 'It's funny, the harder I practise, the luckier I get'. Luck is best defined as where preparation meets opportunity.

3 Self-discipline

As W. Clement-Stone says, 'Self-discipline is the master key to riches'. The best time to develop self-discipline is in advance of when you really need it. Napoleon was quoted as saying 'The strong man is the one who is able to intercept at will the communication between the senses and the mind'.

4 Continuous personal development

Regardless of your field of endeavour, always keep growing, learning and developing. Two very practical things you can start to do are to:

▶ Read for 30-60 minutes every day, ideally first thing in the morning

▶ Listen to tapes when you are travelling.

5 Plan every day in advance

Most people claim to do this, and yet are still frustrated at their level of effective time management. Try this: Everyday rewrite your goals and objectives. Firstly, review your long-term goals (two-three years), then break them down into short-term goals (two-three months) and then weekly and daily goals, before you start any to-do lists; that way you will find it much easier.

6 Set priorities on your time and activities

Until you value your time more, you will never learn to manage it better. The essence of effective time management is that there is always enough time to do the most important things, if you can decide what they are.

7 Exercise

145

An essential quality of nearly all successful people is their abundance of energy and enthusiasm. High levels of personal energy and enthusiasm are a direct benefit of being physically fit. We can achieve and maintain a good level of fitness by combining a sensible diet with regular aerobic exercise of between 30-60 minutes, three times a week.

8 Create thinking time

Sit somewhere quietly without interruptions, or go for a peaceful walk, for about 20-30 minutes. Do this regularly and you will be amazed at its effectiveness. You will begin to look forward to this 'processing' time, indeed to rely on it. You will begin to get new ideas, see things from different perspectives and deal with stress and problems more easily than you thought possible.

9 Ask these two questions after every event:

► What did I do right?

► What would I do differently?

Whilst very simple, they have a tremendous way of maintaining self-esteem by recognising what you did right, and giving you control over your mistakes.

10 Treat everyone as your most important customer

Whether you're in business or not, or whether it is a potential customer or not, just treat everybody with the importance, courtesy, attention and respect you would show to someone who has come to you personally to spend £1m. Remember, you never know...

'Not everything that is faced can be changed, but nothing can be changed until it is faced.'

JAMES BALDWIN

101 Ten ways to get your own way

Every hour of everyday, at every level in every organisation, influential people succeed and non-influential people don't. Every outstanding business contains more than its share of influential people. So here's how you do it:

1 Make a good first impression

It is almost a cliché, but it is also true that you never get a second chance to make a first impression. So don't turn up to a meeting in that bright green Nylon leisure suit if you want to be more influential. The first few seconds in any encounter can make the difference between success and failure, no matter what happens afterwards. Take care with dress and appearance. When they first meet you, people draw conclusions from your carriage, clothing, attitude, voice, tone, handshake and eye contact. They also notice when you smile!

2 Depth of knowledge

Get to know everything you can about your business. Develop two kinds of knowledge: fingertip knowledge – the knowledge you always have at your fingertips; and resources knowledge – knowing where to go or who to ask to get the right answers.

147

3 Breadth of knowledge

Know a little about a wide variety of subjects, so that there's always something you can talk about with someone else. Breadth of knowledge comes from experience and wide reading. The quickest way is to read a good newspaper every day.

4 Sense of humour

Don't necessarily be the office joker, but never take yourself too seriously either. If you are prepared to laugh at yourself, then people will respect and respond to your evidence of self-esteem.

5 Big picture detail

An apparent contradiction, but essential, influential people have the ability to see the big picture while also concentrating on details and carrying little things through to a conclusion. Nobody said it was easy!

6 Versatility

This is the ability to modify your behaviour. Be flexible in dealing with people. Never 'go by the book'.

7 Enthusiasm

You need to be excited about what you are doing. If you are not interested or enthusiastic, you won't so much influence people as put them to sleep.

8 Self-esteem

People can tell whether you're comfortable and happy with yourself. If you're not, why should they be? One way to develop self-esteem is through using these ten influencing skills.

9 Willingness to take risks

The safe way is not always the right way. Nobody ever got ahead without taking risks. 'Be where the bombs are falling and dance like hell!'. Don't let your business become safe. Make it a place where people feel good about trying new ideas.

10 Creativity

A good definition of creativity is 'The juxtaposition of ideas which were previously thought to be unrelated'. Creativity is what drives businesses forward. Invite and encourage creativity throughout your organisation but accept that making mistakes is one of its most common side effects. Not that there's anything wrong with mistakes, of course.

102

Two ears and one mouth

'Why do people have two ears and only one mouth?'

Because listening is twice as important as talking, the best managers, sales people, leaders (and lovers for that matter) all listen more than they talk. Then, when they do talk, they make sense and other people listen.

103 Assume you have absolute authority

Next time you think about doing something, don't worry and waffle, just assume that you have absolute authority and do it.

Then keep on acting this way until somebody tells you otherwise. If you try to derive your authority and freedom of action from any other source than yourself, you will achieve less than you are able. Powerlessness is a state of mind.

Always act with honesty, integrity and congruity. Aim to do the 'right' thing and at all times. We often know instinctively what this is, but it is our logical mind that interferes and confuses issues.

Encourage everyone in your business, team and household to do the same. Instead of delegating complex instructions, ask people to do whatever they feel is best, and the best job they possibly can do.

As an example, one major global hotel chain replaced a detailed customer service manual with a simple plastic laminated card that was issued to all staff. It bore the inscription 'Always act in the best interests of the long-term customer'. They no longer had to refer to the manual, check with managers for authority or worry about being criticised. Instead of giving away the profits, they worked out much more creative ways of achieving customer satisfaction.

'It is more practical to beg forgiveness than to seek permission.'

04 Don't just get promoted, get famous

What do you want to be famous for?

Work out the answer to this question for yourself and set out achieving it. Everyone needs an alter-agenda; a higher goal they're heading for which transcends everyday work.

Make sure that instead of trying to win favour or manoeuvre yourself politically you create real achievements and measurable value.

Instead of getting known by a few, influential managers, get known by as many people as you can – inside and outside your enterprise. Welcome opportunities to speak or discuss issues with the media and business.

Most importantly though, make sure that you do things and associate yourself with projects, task and activities that are visible, appreciated and have an impact on your organisation.

105 Be a winner, not a loser

Here are ten examples of the differences between a winner and a loser:

1   A winner makes mistakes and says, 'I was wrong'. A loser says, 'It wasn't my fault'.

2   A winner credits his good luck for winning even though it wasn't luck. A loser credits his bad luck for losing, even though it wasn't luck.

3   A winner works harder than a loser and has more time. A loser is always 'too busy'; too busy staying a failure.

4   A winner goes through a problem and a loser goes around it.

5   A winner shows they are sorry by making up for it. A loser says they are sorry but does the same thing the next time.

6   A winner knows what to fight for and what to compromise on. A loser compromises on what he should not and fights for what is not worth fighting for. Everyday is a battle of life and it is very important that we are fighting for the right things and not wasting our time with trivia.

7   A winner says, 'I'm good, but not as good as I ought to be'. A loser says, 'Well, I'm not as bad as a lot of other people'. A winner looks up to where they are going. A loser looks down at those who have not yet achieved the position they have.

8   A winner respects those who are superior to them and tries to learn from them. A loser resents those who are superior to them and tries to find fault with them.

9   A winner is responsible for more than their job. A loser says, 'I only work here'.

10 A winner says, 'There ought to be a better way of doing it'. A loser says, 'Why change it – that's the way it's always been done'.

'If you're not fired up with enthusiasm, then you might end up being fired with enthusiasm.'

153

10**6** Be positive

'Attitude' is critical to any outstanding business. What is a PMA (Positive Mental Attitude)? Consider a water jug with the level at the halfway mark:

▶ To a positive person it is half full

▶ To a negative person it is half empty.

What does this really mean?:

▶ Positive people see opportunity in adversity

▶ Negative people think the grass is brown on both sides of the fence!

Think about these examples:

1a I've tried but people just don't want to buy – people just don't want it.

b So far I've not been able to sell this product. But I know it's good and I'm going to keep going until I find the formula.

2a Competition has all the advantages – how do you expect me to sell against them?

  b Competition is strong that's true – but no one ever has all the advantages – lets put our heads together and find a way to beat them.

3a The problem is too great; it's impossible to solve.

  b It's not a problem, it's a situation and a solution does exist – all we have to do is find it.

4a It's no use, we're beaten.

  b We're not beaten yet – lets keep trying – here's a new idea.

5a It won't work – let me prove it.

  b It will work – let me prove it.

6a The market is saturated – 75 per cent of the potential is already filled by other companies.

  b 25 per cent of the market is wide open – let's get started – this looks exciting.

155

'Success comes in "cans" not "cannots".'

107 Don't waste energy worrying and blaming

Worrying and blaming says, 'I'm not in charge'. A major cause of business failure is complaining instead of creating.

During the Apollo 13 flight commanded by Jim Lovell, there was an explosion on board. Immediately afterwards Lovell spoke to Houston and said a phrase which has become almost as famous as the Apollo flights themselves, he said:

'Houston, we have a problem,' and everyone at Mission Control, on hearing that knew that Jim Lovell was in charge of Jim Lovell. What would you have said? How would you have reacted? There you are up there in a spacecraft built by the lowest bidder and part of it explodes!

The overwhelming natural tendency is to worry about it; to blame others, but Lovell and the hundreds of other people involved kept their minds focused on solving the situation, which they did.

We can all learn from this; we each have a certain amount of creative energy – we can either waste it worrying and blaming others or we can focus it on solving business set backs.

When things go wrong we should each ask ourselves: 'Am I part of the problem?' or 'Am I part of the solution?'.

And finally, resist the temptation to tell others your problems – half of them don't care and the other half are glad!

*'Life's battles don't always go
To the stronger or faster man,
But sooner or later the man who wins
Is the man who thinks he can.'*

157

108 Cultivate the habit of going the extra mile

Be willing to do more than is either expected or required. Give extra service happily, whether to your staff, their families, your managers, shareholders, suppliers or customers. The person who does more than he is paid for, is soon willingly paid more.

Ask yourself: 'How can I increase my service today?'.

For a short time we may find we are worth more than we get, but the two will eventually match up – they have to.

The average employee does just enough work not to get fired, and in return, the average employer pays just enough money to keep people from quitting and on that happy basis they go through life!

'Folks who never do any more than they get paid for never get paid for any more than they do.'

ELBERT HUBBARD

109 When in doubt – think what a failure would do and do the opposite

Real success is still unusual – achieved by the minority of people – the 80/20 rule applies here too. Therefore, choose your role models carefully; studying the means and methods of the best managers and businesses can teach you a great deal. However, so can examining the worst examples.

Success is not achieved by:

1 Doing what everybody else does.

2 Following our usual likes and dislikes – our usual habits!

3 Being guided by our natural preferences and prejudices.

4 Just doing what comes naturally.

The common denominator of success, the one factor present in every success story is:

Forming the habit of doing what failures don't like to do!

For example, setting goals, planning, working on ourselves, using time efficiently, avoiding frequent coffee breaks and long unproductive lunch hours, cutting down on unnecessary conversations in goal achieving time with people who are neither prospects or customers.

The common denominator of success can be used to overcome difficult business situations. Think what a failure would do in the same circumstances and do the opposite!

'The three great essentials to achieve anything worthwhile are first, hard work; second, stick-to-itiveness; third, common sense.'

THOMAS A. EDISON

10 Decide to be outstanding

Have you ever thought about the thousands of people who say, 'I'm searching for myself' – who feel they have great potential but just don't know what it is?

They read books on how to discover the 'self'. They go to vocational guidance searching for what will develop this potential. But they never find it because nothing is there! That's what people find when they search for the 'self' – nothing.

The 'self' is not found, it is created. We don't discover our potential; we decide on it and then go to work developing it. People become excellent by first deciding they are going to be excellent, then doing something about it. So, to discover our greatest potential – the one thing we are really good at – here's what to do:

DECIDE!

Decide what we are going to be excellent at and then go to work developing it. We can get there faster by continuously asking ourselves:

'If I were the top man in my business, how would I handle this?'.

161

'Life is a battle from the beginning to the end. One of the biggest battles you will ever have will be with yourself.'

DR NORMAN VINCENT PEALE

111 Be a progressive thinker

Think progress. Believe in progress. Push for progress. Everything around us is growing. We can't stand still; we can either move forwards with it or drop back. It is impossible to be in business today, use yesterday's skills and expect to be in front tomorrow.

Eight ideas for being a progressive thinker:

1   Don't let tradition – 'Why change it, that's the way it's always been done' – stagnate your mind. Instead experiment – try new approaches.

2   Become a 'How can I do it better?' person. When you ask yourself this, your creative power is switched on. Remember the phrase: Good, better, best, never let it rest, until your good is better and your better is best!

3   Ask yourself 'How can I do more?'. Capacity is a state of mind.

4   Eliminate 'Impossible', 'Won't work', 'Can't do it', from both your speaking and thinking vocabulary when appraising new ideas.

5   Become an enthusiast for your profession. Thousands start a new job and wait for the job to prove itself to them. It never will, the job couldn't care less. It's unimportant when we get into the business, what matters is when the business gets into us.

6   Ask yourself if you were an outside investor, would you invest in you?

7   S-T-R-E-T-C-H your mind. Associate with people who can help you think of new ideas and new ways of doing things. Mix with people of different social and business interests.

8   Remember, a mind that feeds only on itself rapidly becomes under-nourished and incapable of creative thought.

'Imagination is more important than knowledge.'

EINSTEIN

112 Don't ever quit

Making mistakes in business is inevitable. A man who says he has never made a mistake has never done anything. However, there is one mistake you must never make. Don't quit.

Don't Quit

When things go wrong, as they sometimes will,
When the road you're trudging seems all uphill,
When the funds are low and the debts are high,
And you want to smile, but you have to sigh,
When care is pressing you down a bit –
Rest if you must, but don't you quit.
Life is queer with its twists and turns,
As everyone of us sometimes learns,
And many a fellow turns about
When he might have won had he stuck it out.
Don't give up though the pace seems slow –
You may succeed with another blow.
Often the goal is nearer than
It seems to a faint and faltering man;
Often the struggler has given up
When he might have captured the victors cup;
And he learned too late when the night came down,
How close he was to the golden crown.
Success is failure turned inside out –
The silver tint of the clouds of doubt,
And you can never tell how close you are,
It may be near when it seems afar;
So stick to the fight when you're hardest hit –
It's when things seem worst that you mustn't quit.

ANON

'Quitters never win

Winners never quit.'

VINCE LOMBARDI

165

113 Learn to really listen

There are some skills or techniques you can use to implement active listening. These include:

1 Repeat back of information

2 Restatement of meaning (rephrasing)

3 Reflection of feeling

4 Questioning for clarification

5 Encouraging the speaker

6 Summarising the conversation

7 Tolerating silences.

Looking at each of these techniques individually:

1 Repeat back of information

You will encounter a number of situations where what you want to do is to verify certain kinds of information, for example:

▶ More details about something

▶ Quantities and examples

▶ Dates and data for follow-up actions.

In cases such as these, you need to repeat – word for word – what has been said. Your purpose in using this technique is to make certain that the information you've received is accurate.

2 Restatement of meaning (rephrasing)

On other occasions, your primary interest is in the communication of meaning. When people say something, the meaning you get may be quite different from the meaning they intended. The technique of restatement is simply using your own words to give your people feedback on the meaning you receive.

It is important that you do not confuse the technique of restatement with the technique of repeat back. Nothing will annoy your people more than constant 'parroting'.

3 Reflection of feeling

This technique is especially useful when dealing with people who are angry or in some other highly emotional state. Often these emotions persist until the person experiencing them recognises that their emotions are being acknowledged. For example:

'That must be very frustrating.'

When you acknowledge people's emotional state, you let them know they are being heard. This will allow you to zero in on the problem causing the emotion.

4 Questioning for clarification

Another way to check on someone's meaning is by asking questions. You can also use questions simply to probe for more information.

The important thing to remember about questions is that they are used as a tool to obtain additional information to clarify your understanding of the person's situation.

Questions can be used to:

▶ Get a clearer definition of a problem

▶ Obtain specific information

▶ Determine what might be causing the problem.

5 Encouraging the speaker

Encouraging statements are very appropriate when you want to keep someone talking. Encouraging people to talk can take several forms. You might say something indicating your interest in what they have to say i.e. 'I'd like to hear about that'.

You might use simple bridging techniques. i.e. 'That's interesting. Tell me more about that'.

6 Summarising the conversation

You will find that periodically summarising the points made in conversations with people is one of the most useful communication techniques of all.

Summarising them:

▶ Provides you and the other person with a summary of what has been agreed or discussed

▶ Allows you both to establish consensus on what has been discussed

▶ Allows you to change the direction of the conversation.

7 Tolerating silences

Bite your tongue! That's what this technique is all about. There are times in every conversation when you need time to think, such as:

▶ You're asked a tough question

▶ You have asked someone a question.

Because time seems so extended during periods of silence on the telephone, you'll probably find yourself wanting to comment or continue the conversation before the other person is ready to do so.

Remember, the first person to speak loses. When people need time to think, let them have it.

14 Questioning techniques

To obtain accurate and complete information and to work coopera-
tively with people, you must use the technique of questioning or probing.
Here are some useful skills:

Probing

Probing is questioning to obtain the specific information you need to
solve problems effectively, to answer questions, or to progress a sale.
Why probe? By probing, you can find out quickly:

► If there is a problem, what the people think the problem is. (You
should remember that someone's idea of a problem is often right.
But sometimes, their own ideas or actions may be part of the
problem.)

► Clues to the cause of a problem. (Many factors can be responsible for a problem – the person, the salesperson, clerical staff,
events, actions – in summary a combination of people and events.)

► Facts to help you to research. (These may include dates or invoice
numbers or other information to help solve the problem, answer
the enquiry, or make a sale.)

169

Once you obtain the information you require by probing, you can use
it to help solve a problem, clarify a situation, or gain commitment to
your suggestions or ideas.

Types of probe

There are two kinds of questions you can use to probe: open-ended
questions and closed questions:

Open-ended questions
► An open-ended question encourages people to give you a lot of
information. When you use open-ended questions, you provide
people with the opportunity to give you the information as they
choose.

▶ Key words for open-ended questions are: 'who', 'what', 'when', 'why', 'where' and 'how'.

Closed questions

▶ A closed question demands a 'yes', 'no' or a limiting answer. When you use a closed question, you direct the conversation to the specific information you require.

Using probes

There are various occasions that call for probes with open-ended questions:

Open-ended questions

▶ To bring out a lot of information with a few questions early on in a conversation. It would take many more closed questions to obtain the same information as one or two open-ended questions. For example: 'What seems to be the problem?'.

▶ To obtain an understanding of the person's real situation. Open-ended questions encourage someone to answer in detail and they are less threatening than closed questions.

▶ To extract a detailed answer after closed questions have directed you to the information you want to know. For example: 'Why not?'.

There are occasions where closed questions are called for:

▶ To clarify a point

▶ To redirect a wandering conversation

▶ When someone volunteers very little information.

Probing helps you to obtain the facts immediately. The sooner you know the facts, the quicker you can answer the query, solve the problem or make your sale.

15 Life lessons

Only a fool believes that he or she makes no mistakes and it's a bigger fool who makes the same mistake twice. Identify your mistakes, analyse them, relish them and learn from them. Turn failures of the past into successes of the future.

If you're not making enough mistakes or failures, then you might not be trying to achieve hard enough.

'Failures and setbacks come to instruct, not to obstruct.'

BRIAN TRACY

171

116 The argument against arguments

Winning an argument is no great achievement. Avoiding one requires far more skill. Neutralise acidic conversation by asking questions rather than making assertions. With practice, you'll become so experienced that your 'opponent' will reach your point of view and believe that it was their idea in the first place.

17

Self-reference is no reference

Avoid egocentric language. However modestly meant, it gives the impression of arrogance. Avoid expressions beginning 'I think...', 'In my opinion.' and 'If I were you'. Keep your personality in the background. Make your customer, boss, colleague, child, friend or lover the reference in your conversation. Every time you want to say 'I', try saying 'You' instead.

118

Asked any good questions?

Physicist Isidor Rabi, who won a Nobel prize in the 1930's for inventing a technique that permitted scientists to probe the structure of atoms and molecules, attributed his success to the way his mother used to greet him when he came home from school each day: 'Did you ask any good questions today Issac?' she would say.

19 Just do it

Quick and dirty. Just do it. Don't polish it, or wait for perfect conditions, or keep on fiddling with a job or a memo or a report until it's too late. Get the job done. Then once it's done, don't waste time worrying about it. Get on to the next job and then the next; you'll double your output.

How to tell if you are indecisive: if you have piles of paper on and around your desk.

Each document in your in-tray is a decision not yet made. Try this: have days of instant decisions. Don't wait for more information. Don't consult with anyone – just decide. Chances are, your instant decisions will be just as effective as the ones you've pondered for weeks.

120 How to use averages to achieve more than the average

A very successful business leader once said that, on average, only one decision in three that he made turned out right.

For most of us, such an average would scare us into never making a decision again. We'd have two failures for every success, so we'd try to stay safe by never committing ourselves again!

But decisions must be made and it is well-known that the most successful people are the ones who make more of them. So our famous business person took a leaf out of the professional baseball player's book and started thinking in terms of averages. His 'correct decision average' was 33%, so instead of worrying that he had a 2:1 chance of being wrong every time, he changed his attitude and told himself that he made one third of a correct decision, every time he made one. Fired by this new frame of mind, he was able to approach every decision with enthusiasm, knowing that each one was one third of a roaring success.

'Courage is the first of human qualities because it is the quality that guarantees all the others.'

WINSTON CHURCHILL

21 Don't be a jack of all trades

If you hold a magnifying glass over a newspaper on a hot summer's day, with the right focus, you can start a fire. However, keep moving it around and nothing will happen.

Think about the business people, sports stars, musicians, artists, teachers and professionals who you consider excellent or are at the top of their profession. They may or may not have god-given or genetic talent. However, they will all have dedicated themselves to their trade, skill, hobby or passion.

Strengths in one area or in a few skills are usually balanced by weaknesses in others. The brilliant salesperson may struggle with paper-work reports; the genius cook with time-keeping; the motivator and communicator with attention to detail.

Merit and reward goes to those individuals and enterprises who can do things excellently, not averagely. Tolerate faults and imperfections in yourself and others – it is usually a price worth paying.

177

'Do what you do, and do it well. Don't try and do a bit of everything.'

OSCAR WILDE

122 Variety is the spice of life

If you're feeling jaded, tired or bored, try a little variety. You'll be surprised at how even an insignificant change in your routine can change your life. Change your breakfast cereal. Move your desk. Make your mouth smile. Loosen up. Wear your beach shirt to work.

'Consistency is the last resort of the unimaginative.'

OSCAR WILDE

123 Stop 'municating'

Despite of all the advantages and benefits of using e-mails, they are no substitute for eye-to-eye or ear-to-mouth conversations. Unfortunately we seem to be developing the habit of 'municating' – simply broadcasting out.

Learn to recognise the issues and people where communicating is required; where discussion will achieve more than dictates, or where conversation is better than blind copying.

The one thing that truly marks humans out compared to other animals on this planet is our ability to communicate the way we do.

124 Managing to be remembered

Try this now. Imagine you're leaving your company tomorrow. What do you want people to say about you? What would you want your ex-colleagues to remember you for? Now write it down and set about achieving it. People won't be able to believe your new vigour and dynamism.

25 Be positive for a day

There's a well-known story about two footwear salesmen who are sent to a Pacific Island with instructions to report back by telegram. One salesman goes to the north of the island, the other to the south. The first telegram reads 'Bad news, the natives don't wear shoes'. The second reads 'Good news, the natives don't wear shoes'.

Tomorrow, be totally positive all day long (or for as long as you can). Eliminate negative phases from your speech, greet people with a smile, and be enthusiastic about your colleagues and friends. They'll respond with positive behaviour of their own and you will have made the best use of everyone's abilities.

126 Be passionate in business

In the entire history of the human race, there has never been any such thing as a dispassionate innovator.

The only thing that all successful people have, whether they are parents or politicians, teachers or programmers, managers or salespeople is a passion for what they want to achieve.

For example, if you are going to set up your own business, choose something that you are really fascinated and impassioned about; something that you can be outstandingly enthusiastic about. Not only will you have a better chance of being good in this area, but you will also find the long hours are more play than work. Convincing others of your ideas and propositions will also be easier.

27 Slow down and achieve more

▶ **Do you dash around all day?**

▶ **Do you panic easily?**

▶ **Do you get flustered when you don't have time to finish a job?**

Try this. Everyday, make at least one conscious effort to slow down all body movements. Make everything deliberate and slow. Don't move unless you have to, try to sense your mind becoming clearer. If you can, establish this habit of slow movement as a regular part of your daily routine and you could well find that the next time you feel the need to rush or panic it won't be quite so overpowering.

128 The only people in the world

Keep telling yourself this: there are only two kinds of people in the world who pay your mortgage for you: customers and rich relatives. Customers are easier to get.

29 High-impact questions

High-impact questions maximise any communication where persuasion and influence is required, by returning high-value information in an efficient amount of time. They can also be used to get people to come around to your way of thinking. Once you are familiar with these high-impact questions, decide on the statement or viewpoint you would like the person to state and then create the questions to lead them there.

High-impact question = high value information and persuasion.

High-impact questions get people to think, organise information, and search for new meanings to existing information before responding. They ask them to:

▶ Evaluate or analyse

▶ Speculate

▶ Express feelings

▶ React.

The result is the type of information you might hear if you were to attend a customer's problem solving or planning session. Good high-impact questions make people say:

'… I don't know. I never thought about that.'

'Hmm… I never put those ideas together that way before.'

Criteria

High-impact questions should be:

▶ Brief and clear

▶ Open-ended

▶ Phrased to require a thoughtful answer

▶ Relevant to the customer's situation and position.

Using high-impact questions in sales calls has several benefits to you. High-impact questions are likely to:

▶ Involve the customer by requiring him or her to think

▶ Increase the amount of time that the other person talks

▶ Provide new insights into problems

▶ Produce high-quality information

▶ Expose underlying issues

▶ Result in yourself being seen as a perceptive individual who can function as a consultant

▶ Cause the person to believe that the conversation was valuable.

Comparison to open-ended questions

Open-ended questions invite people to respond with more than a 'yes' or 'no' answer. However, open-ended questions may elicit factual information that could easily be found in files, annual reports, or organisational charts.

People who enjoy talking about their organisations or themselves may respond willingly to open-ended questions for a while, since it allows them to talk. However, such conversation does not usually require them to engage in high-level thinking, nor is it likely to produce any new insights of value for them.

Tips on high-impact questions

▶ Prepare high-impact questions to use with a person as part of your conversation.

▶ Once in front of them, you may use these prepared questions or devise others spontaneously in response to points they have raised.

Encourage the person

High-impact questions are tough to answer. If you do not encourage while questioning, the customer may feel interrogated. By encouraging frequently, you can take the edge off your high-impact questions and make the section more conversational.

Examples of high-impact questions

Evaluate or analyse
- ▶ How would you compare X with your Y?
- ▶ How would you evaluate your ability to…?
- ▶ What are the three most important difficulties you face…?

Speculate
- ▶ What does the trend in … mean to your…?
- ▶ If you could improve …, what would it look like?
- ▶ Suppose you could …?
- ▶ What if …?
- ▶ How about…?
- ▶ What would be the impact of…?

Express feelings
- ▶ What else do you feel is important?
- ▶ How do you feel about …?

React(ive)
- ▶ How will … impact … specifically?
- ▶ How would you react to the statement …?

187

Asking difficult questions

Some questions may be challenging to ask because they are personal, controversial, or direct in nature. One way to ask difficult questions is with the supported question format:

Reason + Benefit + Question

A supporting statement braces a difficult question with the reason for the question and the benefit to the customer of responding; this format helps you to earn the right to ask the difficult question.

'If they say it they believe it, if you say it they question it.'

130 Get a life

Lee Iococa, Head of Chrysler and one of the greatest business talents of his generation, is on record as saying, 'compared to my family, my business achievements are insignificant'. Take time for the things that really matter; get a sense of perspective, live each day to the full and that means not making it all work.

189

Hawksmere publishing

Hawksmere publishes a wide range of books, reports, special briefings, psychometric tests and videos. Listed below is a selection of key titles.

Desktop Guides

The company director's desktop guide *David Martin* • £15.99

The company secretary's desktop guide *Roger Mason* • £15.99

The credit controller's desktop guide *Roger Mason* • £15.99

The finance and accountancy desktop guide *Ralph Tiffin* • £15.99

The marketing strategy desktop guide *Norton Paley* • £15.99

The sales manager's desktop guide
Mike Gale and Julian Clay • £15.99

Masters in Management

Mastering business planning and strategy *Paul Elkin* • £19.99

Mastering financial management *Stephen Brookson* • £19.99

Mastering leadership *Michael Williams* • £19.99

Mastering marketing *Ian Ruskin-Brown* • £22.00

Mastering negotiations *Eric Evans* • £19.99

Mastering people management *Mark Thomas* • £19.99

Mastering personal and interpersonal skills *Peter Haddon* • £16.99

Mastering project management *Cathy Lake* • £19.99

Essential Guides

The essential guide to buying and
selling unquoted businesses *Ian Smith* • £29.99

The essential guide to business planning and raising finance
Naomi Langford-Wood and Brian Salter • £29.99

Business Action Pocketbooks

Edited by David Irwin

Building your business pocketbook	£10.99
Developing yourself and your staff pocketbook	£10.99
Finance and profitability pocketbook	£10.99
Managing and employing people pocketbook	£10.99
Sales and marketing pocketbook	£10.99
Managing projects and operations pocketbook	£9.99
Effective business communications pocketbook	£9.99
PR techniques that work	*Edited by Jim Dunn* • £9.99
Adair on leadership	*Edited by Neil Thomas* • £9.99

Other titles

The John Adair handbook of management and leadership
Edited by Neil Thomas • £29.95

The inside track to successful management
Dr Gerald Kushel • £16.95

The pension trustee's handbook (2nd edition)	*Robin Ellison* • £25
Boost your company's profits	*Barrie Pearson* • £12.99
Negotiate to succeed	*Julie Lewthwaite* • £12.99
The management tool kit	*Sultan Kermally* • £10.99
Working smarter	*Graham Roberts-Phelps* • £15.99
Test your management skills	*Michael Williams* • £12.99

The art of headless chicken management
Elly Brewer and Mark Edwards • £6.99

Exploiting IT in business
David Irwin • £12.99

EMU challenge and change – the implications for business

John Atkin • £11.99

Everything you need for an NVQ in management

Julie Lewthwaite • £19.99

Time management and personal development

John Adair and Melanie Allen • £9.99

Sales management and organisation   *Peter Green* • £9.99

Telephone tactics   *Graham Roberts-Phelps* • £9.99

Business health check   *Carol O' Connor* • £12.99

Customer relationship management   *Graham Roberts-Phelps* • £12.99

Hawksmere also has an extensive range of reports and special briefings which are written specifically for professionals wanting expert information.

For a full listing of all Hawksmere publications, or to order any title, please call Hawksmere Customer Services on 020 7824 8257 or fax your details on 020 7730 4293.